# THE TIME CRUNCH

Mastering Ministry's Pressure Points

# THE TIME CRUNCH

## What to Do When You Can't Do It All

STEVE MCKINLEY
JOHN MAXWELL
GREG ASIMAKOUPOULOS

MULTNOMAH BOOKS

THE TIME CRUNCH

published by Multnomah Books
*a part of the Questar publishing family*

© 1993 by Christianity Today, Inc.

International Standard Book Number: 0-88070-555-8

*Cover Illustration by Mike Benny*

Printed in the United States of America

Scripture quotations are from the Holy Bible: New International Version
© 1973, 1978, 1984 by International Bible Society
use by permission of Zondervan Bible Publishers

93 94 95 96 97 98 99 00 01 02 — 10 9 8 7 6 5 4 3 2 1

# Contents

## Part 4
## Time to Rest

# Introduction

---

The timer rings. A colorful skier leaps onto the downhill course and accelerates toward the first slalom gate. A digital clock in the upper right hand corner of the television screen measures his performance in blurred hundredths of seconds.

That clock is his biggest opponent, and the announcer won't let viewers forget it. "He has to finish this race in less than one-twenty-two to have any chance of winning the gold!"

Veering from gate to gate, fists punching the fiberglass poles out of his face, skies scraping loudly in the snow, he plummets madly down the mountain.

"He swung wide around that gate," moans the commentator. "That will cost him."

Seconds later the skier cuts by the last gate and curls into a low tuck.

"It looks like he may make it!" cries the announcer. "It's going to be close. . . ."

Time may not have been measured in hundredths of seconds when I was a pastor, but I knew the pressure of the clock. I raced through most days, even days off. I read fast to get the point in the least amount of time.

Facing the limitations of the day, I sometimes felt torn. In prayer, I felt pressure to study. In study, I remembered someone who needed a visit. While visiting, I thought about my family's need for attention. With the family, I thought about planning the next meeting.

I concentrated on being both effective and faithful but also strained to beat the clock, so much so that occasionally my greatest satisfaction came less from comforting a hurting counselee or crafting a persuasive sermon than from keeping to my schedule. If I could check off every item on my to-do list, the day would be a success. Sometimes the clock became lord.

Time is a ruthless master, forcing pastors into a pace as frantic and headlong as a slalom skier. Is there a way to control the clock rather than be controlled by the clock? How can we make time work for us? Rather than process people in order to save time, is there a way to save time in order better to serve people?

The three authors of this volume have tussled with these questions and more.

### Greg Asimakoupoulos

Greg has the melodic name I love to both spell and pronounce (ah sim ah KO puh lus). Call Greg on the phone, and you hear the smooth, rich voice of a former radio DJ and current announcer for Fuller Institute's *Pastor's Update* and *Meta Facts*.

Like most pastors, Greg learned to handle time the hard way:

"Twelve years of task-oriented ministry had taken its toll. I was battling pastoral burnout, and I was losing. The very week the Allied Forces were claiming victory in the Persian Gulf War, my own spirit was surrendering to battle fatigue. Emotional exhaustion. Physical weariness. Spiritual anorexia."

In theory, if you're exhausted, burned out, you find a way to take a long rest. When Greg proposed his superintendent's idea of a sabbatical, leaders in his church responded with a collective, "You've got to be kidding." So he found creative ways to recharge his batteries without leaving church responsibilities.

He has found equally practical and creative ways to handle the other scheduling challenges faced by pastors.

Greg, who received his M.Div. from North Park Seminary and B.A. from Seattle Pacific University, has had articles published in LEADERSHIP and numerous other magazines. He has been pastor of Crossroads Covenant Church in Concord, California, since 1983.

Greg and his wife, Wendy, have three children: Kristin, Allison, and Lauren.

### John Maxwell

When I was in San Diego to interview John Maxwell for these chapters, John confided on the way back from lunch, "I drive a big car because when you get hit it doesn't hurt so bad."

Though he's careful, John is not a timid driver. Nor does he live life or lead a church defensively. He has places to go, and risk is a part of getting there, as is hard work and extraordinary self-discipline.

But John defies categories. He's a straight-ahead, highly organized individual, yet he wrote *Be a People Person* (Victor). From his father, an evangelist and college president, John learned well to relate to people *and* get things done, and he was born as outgoing as any sanguine comes.

John has authored numerous books, including *Be All You Can Be* (Victor), *Deuteronomy* in The Communicator's Commentary series (Word), and *The Winning Attitude* (Here's Life). He is president of Injoy, Inc., a ministry providing tools of motivation and instruction for church leaders.

John received his M.Div. from the Graduate School of Theology at Azusa Pacific University and his B.A. in theology from Circleville Bible College. Before assuming the pastorate of Skyline Wesleyan Church in Lemon Grove, California, in 1981, he served as executive director of evangelism for the Wesleyan world headquarters, and pastored churches in Lancaster, Ohio, and French Lick, Indiana. He and his wife, Margaret, have two children, Sara and Joel.

### Steven McKinley

Steve McKinley looks and sounds like an easy-going guy. He's had reason to be anything but:

"When I came to the church I now serve, congregational morale was in the pits. My predecessor had departed under pressure, a victim of heart troubles during a major building program. The new building was up, but finances were in terrible shape. The congregation was sharply divided over the treatment given to my predecessor; loyal fans and vocal detractors loved to dig at one another. Beyond that, a militant faction at odds with the positions of the Lutheran church kept theological issues stirred up.

"The turmoil dictated the agenda for the first few years. If this congregation was to move forward, the ship had to be stabilized. I had to spend a lot of time listening to unhappy people, helping them work through their anger and grief. I worked diligently with the church council and the finance and stewardship committees, insisting on frugality until we got out of the red."

Steve successfully weathered that tempest. He learned more still about time pressure and time management when the church grew rapidly, which necessitated another building program. Somehow he takes it all in stride, maintaining that easy-going style even in the pressure cooker of pressure cookers: coaching youth baseball.

Steve, who received a B.A. from Augustana College in Illinois and a B.D. from Yale Divinity School, has served in numerous Lutheran leadership, editorial, and writing posts. He wrote *I'm Glad*

*You Asked* (Augsburg Fortress), is a columnist for *Academy Accents*, and writes regularly for LEADERSHIP.

Steve is pastor of Grace Lutheran Church in Andover, Minnesota, where he has served since 1982. Prior to that he pastored churches in Windsor, Connecticut, and Auburn, Massachusetts. He and his wife, Patricia, have three children, Jill, Kirk, and Meg.

Our three authors aren't interested in helping you cross the finish line in world-record time. They agree that the ultimate goal is faithfully and effectively to fulfill one's calling. In the pages that follow, they will help you find the time to do just that.

— *Craig Brian Larson*
*Associate Editor,* LEADERSHIP

*PART ONE*
# Understanding the Internal Clock

---

*I am resisting the lie that more work will make me a better person.*

— *Greg Asimakoupoulos*

# CHAPTER ONE

# The Roots of Busyness

---

The other day my 8 year old expressed her displeasure over the number of times church commitments pirate me away from participating in her bedtime ritual:

"It's not fair, Daddy," Kristin protested. "Can't you call the church and tell them you're busy? Please stay home with us. Let's make popcorn!"

"Tomorrow night, sweetheart," I thought aloud. "I promise. We'll have popcorn *and* root beer floats tomorrow. I don't think I'm busy after dinner."

Her complaint caught me by surprise. I had only recently curtailed my evening appointments to three a week. As I tried to explain the price tag of being a productive pastor, her big brown eyes puddled with tears.

"But Daddy, you're always busy!"

Ouch! That hurt. Kristin's response found an unprotected gap in my priestly armor. But her comment provided me an overdue check on reality.

Was I always busy? And if I was, why?

My daughter's appraisal, I quickly discovered, was correct. When I wasn't preparing to preach, preaching, or spending time with those I preach to, I was preoccupied with ways I could do all three better.

My preoccupation with activity began early on in my ministry. A bachelor pastor for four years, I crowded my life with job commitments, which also doubled to meet my social and emotional needs. My identity was defined by staying busy.

Once I married, though, I thought my eighty-hour-a-week schedule would change. After all, I had an attractive reason to retreat from my study at the end of the afternoon. But it wasn't as easy as I thought.

Even today, when my day off rolls around, my body never seems to notify my mind that sleeping in, riding a bike, catching a movie, or crashing on the couch in front of the TV would be okay. I usually opt for critiquing the previous day's sermon, the organist's performance, wondering why the Whozits weren't in worship, or mentally clearing off my desk.

A typical day finds me arriving home after a nine-hour, non-stop trek. My girls want to tell me about their school days, but my mind is elsewhere. I fight the temptation to reach for the phone, trying to get hold of that person I never could reach during the day.

I zone out at the breakfast table, ordering the subpoints of my sermon more often than I'd like to admit. And when the evening board meeting has gone on past eleven, I've stayed at church to work on a manuscript for a book on a "balanced work ethic" until long after midnight.

Upon reflection I've discovered two primary reasons I tend to stay busy: I'm not a structured person, and I struggle with self-worth.

## Time-Management-Impaired Personality

I'm a creative person who resists structure for structure's sake. I thrive on breathing room.

Consequently, I find it extremely difficult to concentrate on reading or sermon preparation while sitting at my desk at church. I do better in a corner of a restaurant with a bottomless cup of French roast or behind the steering wheel of my car, parked at a scenic lookout high above the city.

In the same way, I need daily "open space" in my schedule. Half of what I end up doing on a given day I hadn't planned to do when I got up. The same is true with other things. I've tried to confine my sermonizing and creative writing to a three-ring binder. But I end up jotting down ideas on the clipboard suctioned to my windshield or the back of a bulk-mail envelope. For me, the creative winds blow where and when they will, and cannot be channeled into prescribed times or places.

I've never been able to get excited about time-management calendars. You know, the ones inviting you to label your daily tasks with an *A*, *B*, or *C* (depending on their importance). Systems with cross-references and index cards leave me feeling as if I'm still learning my preschool *ABC*'s. By the time I've got all my tasks labeled, I don't have any energy or time left in the day to get started.

Creative folks like me aren't always sure which is an *A*, *B*, or *C* task until we start tackling one. Or what initially might appear to be a *C* is transformed into an *A* once a few drops of inspiration fall on it. I don't know how many times I have started using a Daytimer only to give up in frustration several weeks later.

My system is much simpler. I identify the "must-do's" of my week as well as the "want-to's" and try not to allow time for the latter until the former are complete. The must-do's are the obvious: personal nurture, daily family time, sermon preparation, worship planning, staff meetings, mowing my lawn, critical-care calling and vision casting with leadership.

The want-to's are what my creative spirit longs to do: journaling, article writing, attending the symphony with my wife, sending notes of encouragement to people of my parish, composing worship music, taking my daughters to a baseball game, or playing a round of golf with church newcomers.

In spite of my system's simplicity, it's not perfect. I try to do the must-do's first, but I don't always succeed. Sometimes the "What if?" winds give lift to my soul, interrupting my intended flight plan. I've never taken pilot lessons, but the ability to fly by the seat of my pants came naturally to me.

A brainstorm blows by unannounced about how to communicate imaginatively the church budget. My must-do's screech to a halt. I stop what I'm doing, run to the copy machine, enlarge a dollar bill to ten times its actual size, and then mount it on cardboard, slicing it into various widths to represent areas of spending.

I suppose it could wait until next week. But why? Birthing an idea gives me thrust and lift sufficient to keep me aloft when I go back to steer my way through the must-do's. And although I've come to accept operating this way, I have to admit it makes my life less efficient, and therefore more busy, than I often like. In other words, my lack of structure has a dark side.

Quite often Saturday morning comes, and I am not finished with my message for Sunday. I drive over to the church and hole up in my office. I start cranking on my outline.

Then out of the corner of my eye, I notice a pink telephone message slip. I decide to return the call. After all, I need a little break. In making the call, I learn that the person's father died. So next I jot a quick note of sympathy. As I'm about to seal the envelope, I remember that the hymn we will be singing on the morrow speaks to the circumstances of the man's death. I turn on the copy machine, make a copy of the lyrics, and enclose it with the note.

By that time I realize the organist hasn't yet received her copy of Sunday's bulletin. So I drive across town to get it to her. By that time, my daughter's soccer game has begun. Because I allowed my concentration to be interrupted and substituted a should-do and a want-to for a must-do, I was still working on my sermon after supper instead of playing Uno with the family. When I fail to stay with a priority task, I only end up making more work for myself because the must-do's must be done sooner or later. And so, busy, busy, busy; do, do, do.

**Low Self-Esteem**

Charles Hummel says in his popular little booklet, *The Tyranny of the Urgent*, that our greatest ministry danger is letting the urgent crowd out the most important. What he is describing is the third category that complicates my simple system — the "should-do's."

The should-do's are those things others expect the pastor to do. They include hospital calling, visiting in homes, writing visitors, returning phone calls, sitting on standing committees, serving on a denominational task force, teaching a home Bible study, attending the adult-class socials, and playing on the church softball team.

As the word implies, these are activities in which I feel I *should* be involved. There are always should-do's shouted in my direction. In the process of adding so many should-do's to my workweek, however, I end up continually busy, with my emotional tank near empty. In an attempt to catch up, I busy myself to the perishing point. But alas, I never catch up. Only in recent months have I begun to understand why I let others "should" all over me.

Gordon Weekley was a man who worked hard and long as if he had something to prove. He pastored a church of 200 members in Masonboro, North Carolina. Even though it was a stretch, Gordon could make all the hospital visits; he visited in every home; he married, buried, counseled. Gordon never complained about the lousy salary he received. He loved what he did. To him the ministry wasn't a job. Being a pastor was his life.

In Gordon Weekley's biography, *Balm in Gilead: A Baptist Minister's Personal Journey Through Drug Addiction*, author Don Jeffries recounts "the rest of the story." A young rising star in his Baptist denomination, Weekley couldn't lower the RPM's that raced in his head at night. He would lie in bed, worrying about a parishioner in the hospital, a couple with marital conflicts, or how he could craft his sermon just right.

A doctor friend prescribed a tranquilizer. After a while the nightly pill allowing Gordon restful sleep wasn't enough. He discovered a diet pill that provided a rush of euphoria during the day. What began rather innocently as a means of sustaining a thriving ministry nearly destroyed his life. He lost his wife, his four sons, his church, his reputation, and even the control of his own mind.

An underlying poor self-image, it appeared, was to blame. A domino effect was set in motion. As the churches Gordon pastored grew, so did his reputation. So did the demands his members placed on him. So did his ego. The more he satisfied their desires, the more he satisfied his own. It becomes obvious to the reader that Gordon was driven as much by his need to be loved as his love of people.

Although not every goal-oriented pastor plummets to the depths of drug addiction, aspects of Gordon Weekley's story are only too familiar.

For many of us, childhood doubts about our inherent value contaminated the soil of our souls. Subtly taught to fear failure, we were served up conditional love at home, in school, or at church, soon developing a taste for earning acceptance by doing applaudable tasks.

We began to equate busyness with worth. A means of gaining recognition and being affirmed as a person, busyness also has nourished weeds that, in our adult years, now threaten to choke our ministries, marriages, and family life.

In Diane Fassel's book on workaholism, *Working Ourselves to Death*, she connects the workaholic's addiction to low self-esteem: "Because they judge themselves by their accomplishments, they have the illusion they must always be doing something worthwhile in order to feel good about themselves. . . . [Their] sense of self is not separated from their achievements; rather it actually depends upon achievements. Much of [their] frantic activity is symptomatic, an attempt to suppress or deny low self-esteem."

I read Fassel's book in order to review it for a periodical. But as I got into it, I realized I was reading it as much for me as I was for an editor. Much of our busyness — rushing, caring, rescuing — says Fassel, is an attempt to mask the pain associated with the absence of self-worth.

I resonated with those driven by an inner compulsion to perform. It dawned on me that my addiction to achievement and activity had a root system reaching back to innocent days of play, long before I became pastor.

After digesting the book, I grabbed for my journal and, in an attempt to unearth the source of the "shoulds" that control me, started writing. What appeared on paper surprised me:

"I have an instinct deep within that stinks of dead man's bones. I aim too high. I aim to please. I compulsively control. And in the process push away the ones I love, the things I long for, and the wants God has for me. 'Dysfunction' some have called it — a graveyard of my past where my potential birthed by God began to decompose. No longer the sacred ground of being, my life became a cemetery of what might have been. The soil of my survival became the fertile ground of learning how to cope to kill the pain of an impoverished image of my self."

### Digging Up the Roots

Acknowledging the roots of busyness is not sufficient. Action is required. But where to begin?

Sharpening my priorities is not as easy as some gurus of time management imply. For me it will be a challenge every week for the rest of my life. But I am beginning to make peace with the fact that I need not be doing everything I am capable of doing well.

I have also sought help to detoxify my work addiction through therapy. A few months with a Christian counselor improved my "hindsight." He enabled me to see how my neurotic need for approval has dogged me for forty years. My exhausting busyness is an attempt to validate my competency, much like when I held up my kindergarten artwork in front of my parents for their approval. My counselor gave me skills to focus on my own worth and abilities.

Although I have benefited from counseling, the pursuit of self-discipline has been the most logical and painless place for me to begin.

Irwin Hansen, the CEO of Porter Memorial Hospital in Denver, has gained a reputation for turning around medical centers losing money. He has identified "lack of discipline" as culprit number one. Although generating a lot of activity, many hospital employees fail to get their jobs done. His remedy is simple: "All you need is a big pot of glue. You smear some on your chair and some on the seat of your pants. You sit down and you stick with every project until you've done the best you can."

I've had trouble finding my glue jar underneath the to-do piles. But I am making steady progress, structuring for a more disciplined routine. I am attempting, for example, to handle a sheet of paper only once (scanning it, filing it, responding to it, handing it to someone else, or throwing it away) rather than allowing it to join other homeless memos on my cluttered desk.

I'm also finding it helpful to jot down what I need to do on a given day before I get to the office. And by having a typed outline of my message ready for the bulletin (printed on Friday), my sermon is two-thirds done by Saturday morning — so I'm less apt to be sequestered from my family all day Saturday. And as I mentioned in this chapter's opening paragraph, I have voluntarily limited my nights out each week to three.

The practice of self-control is helping me obey the detour sign on my desk. The sign points in the direction of home. I keep it in view to remind me that the "road work" of ministry is never done, but the years of my influence in the lives of three little girls is limited. That little wooden sign calls me to be disciplined in the office so I can leave the office at the office when I go home. Consequently, I'm doing a better job finishing my must-do's. I'm also becoming more aware of what is, in reality, unnecessary. I'm learning a foreign language — the language of saying no.

Most critically, as I discipline myself to reflect on the Scriptures (not for a sermon outline but for my own nurture), I am increasingly exposed to a God who affirms me unconditionally as a human being, not a human doing.

Once again my journal records my hopeful progress:

"Thistles and weeds, seeds I never planted have overtaken my life. I trip. I stumble. I fall flat on my face. But in 'the fall,' I find the guts and grace to get up and walk out of my overgrown graveyard one step at a time."

I am resisting the lie that more work will make me a better person. I am also better able to say "Forget it!" to the should-do's and stick with the must-do's and want-to's. My dependence on other's expectations is slowly being replaced by an increased dependence on what God wants for me.

According to Charles Hummel, this dependence on the Father's agenda is what allowed Jesus always to have time for people and yet never appear stressed: "Jesus' prayerful waiting for God's instructions freed him from the tyranny of the urgent. It gave him a sense of direction, set a steady pace, and enabled him to do every task God assigned. And on the last night he could say, 'I have finished the work which thou gavest me to do.' "

*Time is a remarkably equitable gift.*

— *Steven McKinley*

CHAPTER TWO
# Where Does Time Go?

Before my week started, I knew it was going to be one of those weeks. My appointment book told the coming story: worship services, meetings, classes, appointments, counseling sessions were lined up from Sunday morning through Friday afternoon, like soldiers in an unbroken line. Then, on Friday evening, we would begin the annual twenty-four-hour retreat of our governing board, bringing me home early Saturday evening — only to begin that hectic routine again. On top of that, we were in a building program at the time, and every day I anticipated having to iron out wrinkles and answer questions.

Every morning I was out the door by 7:00. I ate lunch at my desk, dashed home for a quick dinner, and then headed out again, making it home in time only to watch the late-night news and fall asleep in my chair during the weather. By midweek I was feeling frazzled and only semi-prepared for the responsibilities in front of me. Wherever I went, I was constantly aware of the time. I turned into a clock watcher.

On Friday evening at the retreat, I excused myself from the rest of the board members at about 10:00 P.M. to retreat to my room. As tempting as the bed looked, I forced myself to sit down at the desk, for the Sunday sermon was still only in the fetal stages. I pulled my Bible out of my attaché case, and I turned to the page marked with a card. I looked at the card.

"Ted Livingston — heart surgery — Wednesday, 9:00 A.M." it said. I had written myself the note the previous Sunday and stuck it in my Bible. I had forgotten about it until now. There I sat, closeted in a retreat center, having forgotten an essential hospital visit, looking at an unfinished sermon. As busy as I had been all week, I had still missed out on some of the essentials!

Like me, most pastors are busy and frustrated at their inability to get as much done as they would like. They are educated, faithful, loving — they want to be good pastors. But their time is out of control. They are "time bombs."

After struggling with managing time over several decades of ministry, I have learned a few things that have defused time pressure's explosive threat.

### Realistic Assumptions

We all make certain assumptions about ourselves and our time. Unrealistic assumptions make us feel helpless and under the gun. On the other hand, here are five realistic assumptions that ease the pressure.

● *Pastors aren't the only people working long hours.* When tempted to feel sorry for myself, I think of the members of my church council. For the past four months, Harvey, a mechanical engineer, has been directing the start-up of a new machine 150 miles from his home. He leaves home Sunday evening and returns Friday night and assumes he will spend twelve hours a day in the factory.

Todd commutes two hours a day. Mary, a doctor, leaves home at 6 A.M. and considers herself fortunate to get home by 9 P.M. When her beeper goes off during one of our council meetings, she's out the door. Parish pastors do work long, hard hours, but they aren't the only ones.

● *Work will expand to fill the time you give it.* Most jobs require a minimum amount of time to accomplish. At our house, we have an absurdly large yard. Cutting it takes four long hours of riding the mower back and forth, then another hour trimming around the trees and edges with a hand mower. The job can't be done in less time than that.

But we can take more time. If I stop to chat with a neighbor or drink a glass of tea or polish the mower or sharpen the blade, it can take eight hours to cut the grass. If I allow myself eight hours, it will take eight hours.

Writing a sermon, planning a wedding, and talking on the phone to Mrs. Murgatroyd each take a certain amount of time. But if I allow myself more time, the sermon I usually write in four hours can take six. If I take it upon myself to ensure all wedding details are perfect, even those responsibilities of the bride and groom, I can double my preparation time.

● *There is a difference between busyness and accomplishment.* Most pastors are notorious activists, glorying in their jam-packed appointment books. If you're at the local clergy association and agree to lunch sometime with your colleague from St. John's by the Gas Station, it's a thrill to pull out your appointment book and discover you don't have lunch free until three weeks from next Thursday. That filled-up appointment book tells the world you are working hard. Busyness is its own reward.

But you can be busy without getting much done. You can get caught up in trivialities, accept responsibilities that shouldn't be yours, work in a disorganized fashion, and create unnecessary work for yourself.

Decorating our church for Christmas was the speciality of two families in the congregation. They always did a bang-up job. But one December, Nancy was tied up with a new baby, and Harry didn't feel like he could leave her. No problem. Emma and Vern would get the job done.

On her way out the door to come to the church to decorate, Emma slipped on the ice, fell, and broke her ankle. Vern called me from the hospital. He told me that I didn't need to come to the hospital right away, but he also let me know he wasn't up to decorating the church all by himself. He usually came along, he said, just to provide "muscle."

An undecorated church, the decorating committee out of commission — sounds like a job for Super Pastor! The next morning I announced to the church staff that we were decorating the church that day. We turned on the answering machine and charged into the sanctuary.

If I do say so myself, we did a pretty good job. But the price we paid was the time of the entire staff for a whole day one week before Christmas. I had not only done myself in, I had done my colleagues in. I took on a responsibility that should not have been mine and made an already hectic season all the worse.

(By the way, when the next Christmas season came, Emma and Nancy said that the church staff had done such a fine job decorating the church the previous Christmas that they were sure the staff would want to do it again! Once you've accepted a responsibility, it can be very difficult to get rid of it!)

● *You accomplish more than you think.* Pastors are notoriously self-critical. We have high expectations for ourselves, and when we don't meet them, we feel like failures. At the end of the day, we often feel as though we haven't accomplished anything.

That feeling is rarely accurate. I use a yellow legal pad to plan my day. First thing every morning, I pull out the yellow pad. At the top of the page, I write my appointments. On the left side of the page, I list my things-to-do list. On the right hand side, I note the names of people I need to talk to.

As the day goes by, I cross off what's done. Each night I can see how much I accomplished by how much has been crossed off, and it's usually more than I thought.

- *You have as much time as anyone.* Time is a remarkably equitable gift. Whether you are rich or poor, young or old, white or black, male or female, Christian or Jew, you get the same twenty-four hours a day. Nobody gets more. Nobody gets less. The question is how we will manage those hours.

**Where Does Your Time Go?**

If at the end of a long day of ministry your spouse asks what you did all day, you may have a tough time answering. You may say, "I don't exactly know."

We can't control what we don't understand. And I've learned that how we spend our time rarely matches how we think we spend it, and it almost never matches how we ought to spend it.

Here are four steps for changing that.

*1. Write your priorities.* What is most important to you? Preaching? Visitation? Education? Youth ministry? Counseling? Spiritual growth? Study? Family time? Worship? Ecumenical activities? Political action?

Answers to this question will vary based on your personality, gifts, interests, type of congregation you serve, and position. Don't just *think* about those priorities. If it is important to you to make twenty home visits each week or to spend one night each week with your family, write it down. In fact, this is an important principle of effective time management: write it down. Don't trust your memory to hold on to everything you have been told and all of the commitments you have made. *Write them down.* And then put them in your desk for two weeks.

*2. Notice your rhythms.* Are you a morning or evening person? When are your up times of the day, and when are your down times? When do you do your best work?

I'm a morning person. I get to my office before the rest of the staff, before the telephone starts to ring, and before people start stopping by. That gives me quiet time for prayer, study, and planning, when my creative juices are flowing. Early in the morning, I like to write sermons, outline classes, and dream great dreams.

I also know I'm likely to drop into a valley after lunch, to feel sluggish. This is the time to take on routine tasks or jobs so stimulating they overcome my drowsiness. It's time to be moving rather than sitting at my desk. I visit hospitals and shut-ins and make telephone calls in the early afternoon.

Whatever your rhythms, make friends with them.

3. *Examine how you actually spend your time.* Get your hands on a desk-sized personal planner or a professional appointment book. The little pocket-sized appointment books aren't big enough. If you cannot afford that, make a chart of each day broken into fifteen-minute blocks. For the next two weeks, fill in each fifteen-minute block with what you did during that period of time.

Be specific. If the chairperson of the Altar Guild phones to discuss the difficulties she's having scheduling persons to clean up after Communion on Sunday mornings in the summer, write, "Talked with Mrs. Dickinson for thirty minutes about Altar Guild problems," even if some of the conversation was about the weather or this year's tomato crop. But be honest. If you spent fifteen minutes chatting with a neighboring pastor about last Saturday's football game, do not list that as "ecumenical activity."

While you might not want to stop and record your activity every fifteen minutes, don't wait too long. Your memory isn't that good! All this writing might seem like an unnecessary burden, but it's a necessary step toward getting organized. The result will be an accurate record of how you're actually spending your time, enabling you to deal with your real schedule problems, not your imagined ones.

4. *Compare your priority list with how you are actually spending your time.* Pull out of the desk drawer the priorities you developed. Has your schedule been harmonious with your priorities? If visitation is important to you but you only spent two hours in the past two weeks at it, you probably feel frustrated. If preaching is one of your priorities, but you never get around to your sermon until Saturday night, you probably don't feel good about your ministry.

Is the way you spend your time in harmony with the way you believe you should be spending it? If not, you can do one of two things: change your priorities or change your schedule.

## Black Holes of Time

Whether or not I decide to change my priorities, I've got to look for time wasters. Here are some black holes that suck large quantities of my schedule if I'm not careful.

• *Priorities not prioritized.* It's Monday morning. Before the week is over, there's a sermon to write, an article for the newsletter to compose, the agenda for the board meeting to prepare. Mr. Zabel, who is terminally ill, is hoping for a visit, and you haven't been to the nursing home to see Mrs. Terwilliger for several weeks. The Anderson wedding is Saturday, the stewardship committee has asked you to suggest names of prospective calls, and several letters on your desk await response. You should meet with the congregational president before the next board meeting. Your daughter has a softball game on Tuesday night and your son a piano recital on Friday night, and you've agreed to go out to dinner with your spouse *sometime* this week.

Where do you start?

It's time to prioritize. You already have a list of pastoral priorities telling you what's important to you. Rank the week's activities accordingly. Then get out a blank time log for the week and assign them appropriate blocks of time.

Be honest in your scheduling. If it always takes you six hours to write a sermon, don't pencil in only four.

Keep a list of the items that don't fit into your calendar, because you may be able to squeeze them in gaps during the week. Knock off letters one or two at a time. Leave early for your Wednesday luncheon appointment and visit Mrs. Terwilliger. You will get most things done, but you will have made *certain* that you will get *the most important things* done.

• *Attending to too many details.* I have a thing about burned-out light bulbs — can't stand them. If I come into the corridor outside the church offices in the morning, switch on the lights, and the bulb blows, my instinct is to go to the janitor's closet, find the correct light bulb, pull out the ladder, and replace the bulb. Of course, along the way I might remember a burned-out bulb in the third-grade Sunday school classroom, so I replace that one, too. And since I've already got the ladder out, there is that banner over the entrance to the nave that has gotten off-kilter, so I'll straighten it. Then, as I put the ladder back, I'll notice a collection of old bulletins sitting on the shelf in the janitor's closet, so I'll throw them away.

Next thing I know I've been fiddling around for thirty minutes doing jobs that aren't mine. A note to the janitor (thirty seconds to write) would have put him on the trail of these projects and saved me thirty minutes.

It's not that I'm too good to change light bulbs. It's not my job, not the best use of my time. Far better to delegate that task and see to it that he follows through.

● *Staying later and later.* I sometimes envy the people on TV beer commercials. They appear to have put in a solid day's work, but now it's finished. Now they're going to sit back with their friends, enjoy a cold one, and relax in the satisfaction that the day's work is done.

I envy them because I arrive home each night painfully aware of all that didn't get done. No matter how long or how hard I work, I never feel as if I'm completely *done.*

In previous times, we used to hear the saying, "A man may work from sun to sun, but a woman's work is never done." Neither is a pastor's. There's always one more call that should have been made, one more card that should have been sent, one more commentary that should have been consulted. Nonetheless, we run out of hours.

There comes a time to go home, not just to change physical locations but also to leave the day's work behind, letting "the day's own trouble be sufficient for the day." I need to discipline myself to leave the work behind, to enter fully into the life of my family, and to find recreation. On some days quitting time may come at 4:00 P.M. Other days it won't come until 11:00. But when the time comes, I go home.

● *Agreeing to just one more thing.* Awhile back I received a call from Eunice, a woman who is not a member of my congregation. I've worked with her on some community projects; I like and respect Eunice.

After a few preliminaries, we got down to the reason for her call. "Would you be willing to serve on the board of the local humane society? It's just one night a month."

Being a typical pastor, I didn't want to hurt Eunice's feelings. I've learned, however, that most one-night-a-month obligations turn out to be more than that. I am away from home too many nights already, and I attend more than enough meetings to satisfy my meeting urges.

I said no. Eunice pressed her plea, but I held my ground.

Our church is a prime spot for requests to do weddings. We have a prominent location. We have worked hard at doing them right. But a well-run wedding requires a significant amount of my time in premarital counseling, rehearsing, and the actual ceremony. Usually that time is on Friday night and Saturday afternoon, two times I prefer to be with my family, enjoy recreation, or prepare for Sunday morning.

I used to say yes to all the wedding requests we could schedule. But sometimes it was a grudging yes, and I came away frustrated and depressed. Now we say no to most non-member weddings, to those folks who are simply looking for a nice place to get married. I feel bad about that sometimes — but I feel good on Friday night and Saturday afternoon! When I do say yes to a wedding, it's a whole-hearted yes.

It's all right to say no. If we're going to get on top of managing our time, we need to say no intentionally, not by default.

My board once gave me a parody of a famous prayer. As I consider my schedule week after week, I read this:

"God grant me the serenity to prioritize the things I cannot delegate, the courage to say no when I need to, and the wisdom to know when to go home."

*The more we understand our reasons for procrastinating, the better we can develop a game plan to defeat the mañana habit.*

— *John Maxwell*

# CHAPTER THREE

# Overcoming Procrastination

---

I learned my lesson about procrastination early. Every Sunday afternoon of my childhood, my father assigned weekly chores to my brother, sister, and me. Some were daily jobs and others, like sweeping the basement floor, were weekly.

One Sunday Dad set a new policy. "You can do your weekly chores anytime you want. But Saturday afternoon we'll do something as a family. We'll go shopping or swimming or picnicking. But if your chores aren't done by Saturday noon, you won't get to come."

When the next Saturday noon rolled around, my chore wasn't done. My dad kept his word. I watched out the living room window as the family car pulled out of the driveway, and my dad, mom, brother, and sister went for a day at the beach.

We pastors are tempted to put off tough but necessary tasks. We need to confront a member about gossiping, but that could get ugly, so we visit someone in the hospital. We need to propose some cuts to balance the budget, but the tradeoffs will be painful, so we read a book. We need to clarify the church's ministry philosophy, but the more specific we get, the greater the risks appear, so we return phone calls and visit with staff members. We're working, but we're letting important, difficult priorities slide. That's procrastination, and the cost is high.

Procrastination is easy to do, easy to rationalize, and tough to overcome. But even with a sanguine like me, I've learned it can be done.

### Why Mañana?

Reasons to procrastinate abound, some obvious, others subconscious. The more we uncover and understand them, the better we can develop a game plan to defeat the mañana habit. Here are four of the more common causes.

● *Poor self-confidence.* When we know we can do a good job, we can't wait to do it; when we feel inadequate, we procrastinate.

We're poor, say, in administration, so we avoid it every way possible, neglecting even fundamental planning. Or a past failure paralyzes us. Mark Twain said that once a cat sits on a hot stove, it won't sit on a hot stove again. Of course, he said, it won't sit on a cold stove either.

Our failures are the hot stove. You squared off with a stubborn board member at your last church and lost your temper. You forgave him superficially, but bitterness settled in, poisoning your ministry there. Now you're gun-shy of confronting strong personalities. The stakes are too high, the emotions too volatile.

After too many failures, a person won't attempt anything, like the little leaguer who has struck out again and again. Now he just keeps the bat on his shoulder and hopes for a walk, hoping for the pitcher and umpire to get him on base.

The kid who has belted some home runs can't wait to get to the plate and take his cuts. When the game is on the line, he wants to be the hitter. Success breeds confidence and aggressiveness.

New situations can also intimidate us, making us procrastinate — a new church, a building project, a novel program, a counselee with a problem we've never encountered before. When I face things not routine, not habitual, I have to fight consciously the tendency to hold back.

• *Lack of problem-solving skills.* Many pastors who don't normally procrastinate do so in the face of problems. They don't know how to work through problems systematically: how to ask key questions, accumulate pertinent information, create and explore and weigh options, move forward even when the options aren't perfect, and make midcourse corrections.

Building limitations, for example, are one of the most common and intractable problems we face. So naturally, we're inclined to drag our feet rather than begin dealing with the countless details that a building project entails. Since the problem usually doesn't become a crisis, people drift away because of overcrowding or substandard conditions — or they never come back once they've visited.

Problem solving skills, though, can be learned, and such skills are one of the surest ways to liberate a pastor from procrastination.

• *Distaste for certain tasks.* The big three sour balls are confrontation, money, and vision.

No one enjoys confronting others, yet from time to time the church's health depends on it. When I speak at pastors' conferences, pastors regularly say, "I've got a troublemaker in the church. What should I do?"

My first response is "Have you sat with this person one-to-one and talked through the issues?"

Ninety-five percent of the time the answer is no. By avoiding the problem we aggravate it, allowing bitterness to fester, misunderstandings to occur, and falsehoods to spread.

Money issues can leave us in the doldrums, our sails hanging limp. We don't want to drive people away. We want to stay popular. We're sensitive to the jokes about pastors and finances.

At one of my stewardship seminars, a pastor said to me, "Our church is well into a building program, but we're struggling financially. That's because I made a mistake early on. I didn't want to offend anybody, so I 'low-keyed' the finances. We could have easily raised another $75,000 if I had just asked people to make a greater commitment. But I didn't."

Developing vision as a leader seems like something we would gladly embrace, but vision, too, has its down sides. It takes serious prayer, hard work, and intense thought to formulate vision. By choosing one vision, we rule out others just as worthy. Articulating vision means taking risks: everyone in church won't agree on the vision; it will attract some people to our church but repel others. Implementing vision requires a forcefulness we may find uncomfortable.

● *Subject to emotions.* If we follow feelings rather than priorities, procrastination grows. If I wake up asking myself, "Okay, John, how ya' doing, buddy? You ready for the day? What do you think you can handle?" I'll put off many essential tasks, because some days I don't feel like getting much done.

Emotions change; character remains the same. Strong leaders are character based, priority based, rather than feeling based. They forgo gut-check questions, settling that issue when they set their priorities.

Unresolved emotions like anger and guilt also weaken us to the point where we drag our feet. When I came to pastor my first church, I had an early run-in with Joe, a church leader.

Joe's mother painted a picture that hung in the foyer for years. The first time I laid eyes on it, I decided it had to go. I took it down and put it in a closet. Joe didn't say a word. He just retrieved it from the closet and rehung it.

When I noticed it the following Sunday, I asked various people, "Who put the picture back up?" Eventually, Joe admitted, unapologetically, he'd done it.

I stewed for two months about what to do. I knew I had to confront him, but because I was new, I felt insecure in the church. All the while my ego took a beating over backing down and doing nothing.

My feelings not only inhibited my dealings with Joe, they had me so tied in knots I put off other important tasks. Eventually I went to Joe's work and confronted him about it. I didn't convince him of my views, but from then on I was free from anger.

### Thief of More than Time

Someone has called procrastination the thief of time. That's certainly true, but procrastination also steals things far more dear to a pastor.

Putting off ministry tasks is like neglecting maintenance on a new car. If you don't change your oil every 3,000 miles, your car will still start and run. The doors will still open, and the brakes will work. You're getting away with it!

But after 8,000 or 10,000 miles, the engine oil has been saturated with dirt. Those particles are now grinding like liquid sandpaper at the lining of the cylinders, pistons, and rings. Eventually the metal wears away to the point that the car burns oil, the engine knocks. Left unattended, an engine designed to run over 130,000 miles is ready for the junk yard at 80,000 miles.

The cumulative effects of procrastination in ministry are similar. For quite a while you don't see what's happening. But eventually a blue cloud starts billowing behind you.

Here are a few of the costs of doing first things last.

● *We lose productive people.* One pastor I know is an effective preacher but a weak administrator. He has pastored small churches that can't afford secretaries. Although he prepares his sermons well, he usually doesn't get around to organizing announcements or planning worship services until Sunday morning.

His pulpit ministry attracts some sharp people. But when they start working in the church, many grow frustrated with the disorganization and eventually leave.

If we procrastinate, we immediately lose respect from our leaders and activists. Such people are not leaders by accident. They succeed in work and life because they have seized opportunities; they see openings and run for daylight; they size up situations quickly.

When leaders try to work with laissez-faire pastors, they go nuts. They're thinking, *We could have done this. We should have done that.* Eventually they decide the pastor is not going anywhere, so they go elsewhere. The people a procrastinating pastor first loses are the ones he needs most.

● *We squander opportunities.* Opportunities abound for those who do the right thing at the right time. Alfredo Pareto, an Italian economist, first espoused the 80/20 principle of effectiveness. Eighty percent of your productivity, he said, comes from doing well the top 20 percent of your priorities, while only 20 percent of productivity comes from doing the bottom 80 percent of priorities.

Based on this principle, Pareto said to work smarter not harder. Those who work the bottom 80 percent of their priorities but neglect the top 20 percent work four times harder but are only one-fourth as productive as those who work the top 20 percent.

It follows, then, that if we procrastinate on our top 20 percent, we squander our biggest opportunities. It's not only *that* we procrastinate, but *what* we procrastinate. Some pastors pay a much higher price for dallying because of what they dally.

Preparing the Sunday bulletin, for instance, is busy work with little return for a pastor. I have never met anyone who attends a church because of the bulletin, yet every week pastors spend important hours doing something that could be delegated.

● *We lose momentum.* Momentum is one of a pastor's best friends, easily worth five staff members. With it, you're bigger than life. You walk up to the pulpit and say, "Good morning," and everyone says, "He's deep."

Without momentum, or when you experience downward momentum, you're swimming against the current. You say, "Good morning" and people say, "He's shallow."

Procrastination murders momentum. If we drag our feet, we slow the wagon. People excited about starting a new program quickly lose interest if we procrastinate getting them a budget. They may decide never again to take initiative. If we don't get around to calling (or getting someone else to call) the couple that visited last Sunday, they'll likely go elsewhere next Sunday, taking their network of unchurched friends, spiritual gifts, tithe, and winsome personalities with them.

Much of that and the wagon stops, and it's a lot harder to start again.

Decisiveness and prompt action are like the solid fuel boosters that propel the space shuttle into orbit. Doing first things first energizes a church. People sense the can-do faith, the let's-roll-up-our-sleeves-and-go enthusiasm.

● *We lose self-respect.* Pastors can only lose so many productive people, so many opportunities, and so much momentum before they lose their sense of worth.

On the other hand, even if results don't flower immediately, self-regard takes strong root when we do what's difficult, face daunting challenges, smooth rocky relationships, begin solving thorny problems, organize work, and plan a significant future.

### How to Stop Keeping Up with Yesterday

Procrastination is a habit, but we can break it. Here's how to change the attitudes and practices that foster the frustrating art of keeping up with yesterday.

● *List your priorities.* This keeps us from procrastinating where it costs most. Prioritize based on the three *R*'s.

The first *R* is requirements. Ask, *What is required of me? What must I do whether I like it or not? What tasks, if neglected, will cost me leadership, credibility, even my job?*

A pastor decides, *Visiting members in the hospital isn't bearing much fruit.* So instead of visiting members every other day, as he has customarily done and as the previous pastor did, he visits them only once a week, without ensuring that someone else in the church visits them at other times. Before long, people complain, "Pastor Robinson doesn't care about us. He's too busy trying to build himself a big church to take time with the hurting."

So I encourage pastors to sit down with their leaders and ask, "What must I do that no one else in church can do? When is it critical that you see my face and touch my hand?"

When the search committee of Skyline Wesleyan Church interviewed me for the senior pastor position, I asked them what I had to do as senior pastor of Skyline that they would not be willing to have anyone else do. After much discussion we concluded that only I could (1) cast the vision, (2) be the primary preaching pastor, (3) take responsibility for the progress of the church, (4) live a life of integrity as senior pastor, and (5) teach leadership to the pastoral staff.

The second *R* is return. What brings the greatest return to the church? What do I do better than anyone else *that helps the church*?

I'm not talking about just what you do well. You may file better than anyone in church. You may coach basketball better than anyone. But those jobs pay low dividends. What do you do well that significantly benefits the congregation?

My church gets the greatest return when I (1) communicate the vision and direction for the church, (2) equip key people for leadership and strategic planning.

If our first and second *R*'s clash severely, we'll suffer. For example, if the church requires us to begin and maintain an abundance of programs but we're weak in administration, both we and the church will be unhappy. Unless we resolve the tension through give and take, negotiation, and education, such a problem will continue to plague us.

The third *R* is personal reward. We need jobs that we look forward to, that rejuvenate us, that we thank God someone actually pays us to do. Usually these jobs we're good at.

I get the greatest reward from watching people grow, sensing God's presence when I communicate, sharing Christ with others, and developing and equipping people to lead.

After listing your three *R*'s, take all factors into account, weigh the tradeoffs, and prioritize your pastoral tasks.

By the way, procrastination isn't all bad. It's healthy to leave lower priorities undone to ensure we're covering what's most important. Rather than trying to fix everything at once, overcome procrastination in the top 20 percent of priorities and then move down from there.

● *Develop accountability.* When I pastored in Lancaster, Ohio, I decided one of my highest priorities was to model an evangelistic lifestyle for the church. Given my other pastoral responsibilities, that wouldn't be easy, so one December I told the congregation, "Next year I'm going to lead 200 people to Christ. I want you to hold me to that."

A few weeks later on a Saturday night, I went to the church to study and pray for the next morning's service. In the lobby, I met one of our members. "Pastor, I've been praying for you every day," he said, "that God will help you win people to Christ. And every time I pray I wonder how you're doing."

*Good night,* I thought. *I'm done for now.* "Well," I said, "I haven't won anyone yet this week, but there's still time."

Instead of going into my study, I turned around and went to the car. I had one prospect card, Larry and Sue, living on Fair Avenue. I drove to their home, introduced myself, sat down in their living room, and before the night was over they prayed to receive Christ into the center of their lives. They attended church the next day and walked the aisle in a public dedication.

Accountability changes behavior. In the case above, of course, God was gracious enough to allow my effort to be fruitful. In any event, if I had a serious problem with procrastination, I would sit with trusted church leaders and admit my struggle. I would show them my list of priorities and ask if they agreed that those priorities were best for the church. Then I would ask them to hold me accountable for my top priorities.

Often these leaders sense that if you are to handle the top priorities, you will need someone to handle lower priorities. They may, in fact, volunteer to help.

● *Do things that develop confidence.* As a boy I wrestled almost daily with my brother Larry. He always pinned me. He was two years older, strong and husky, and at that time I was literally anemic.

My dad watched Larry pin me over and over, and he saw what it was doing to my confidence. One night he told Larry, "You can't wrestle with John this week. I'm going to wrestle him."

My dad let me win every match. Then he would wrestle Larry and beat him. As I got wins under my belt and saw that Larry was beatable, I gained confidence.

After a week he turned us loose to wrestle again. This time we wrestled to a draw. My brother never pinned me again.

Did I gain strength in one week? No, I gained confidence. And we can gain confidence the same way: by getting small wins under our belts. We can find things (no matter how small) we can succeed at, stay with them long enough for confidence to grow, and then build from there.

Another way to develop confidence is by learning from others. Almost everything I know I learned from somebody.

At my second church we grew beyond anything I had experienced before. We were seating people in the aisles, and frankly, I didn't know what to do. I called up Bob Grey, pastor of a large church in Jacksonville, Florida. "My name is John Maxwell," I said. "You don't know me. I'm a pastor, and I'm coming to Jacksonville on vacation. I need to talk to you. I'll give you a hundred dollars for an hour of your time."

Bob agreed to see me. Several weeks later I walked into his office with a tape recorder, a yellow legal pad, and a list of questions. I punched the recorder and fired away for an hour, asking him about the aspects of ministry that puzzled me most. To correct our overcrowding, the problem I was most concerned about, he suggested two Sunday morning services, a novel idea at that time.

When we were finished, I reached into my pocket and pulled out the check, but he refused it. In fact, he took me out to lunch, and we became good friends.

That went so well, I did the same with other prominent

pastors. These sessions developed my confidence. Not only did I take home pages of great insights that boosted my know-how, their faith-filled attitude rubbed off on me.

• *Develop a problem-solving mindset.* Along with developing the problem-solving skills mentioned earlier, we need continually to nurture a creative attitude. The more creative we are, the more we'll find solutions.

We can learn to be creative. Creativity isn't anatomically fixed in our brains, solely dependent on whether we're dominantly left- or right-brained. It's a way of thinking, an outlook, a habit. We find creative solutions to problems when we (1) think outside of the rigid boxes we're accustomed to, (2) step out of our security zone, and (3) sometimes move forward before we completely figure everything out.

The piano player in a small church moved out of town, leaving the congregation without a replacement. For a few weeks the congregation sang *a cappella*, but people began complaining. "The worship just isn't the same. One off-key person throws everyone off."

The pastor thought about hiring a pianist, but the budget was too tight. So they did nothing, and attendance slowly declined.

How did one Chicago church solve that problem? With worship cassettes available in any Christian bookstore and a boom box. No one had heard of a church worshiping along with a tape, but they tried it. The church grew, and eventually another pianist began attending.

We can't wait till we have all the answers before we start moving. After we take the first creative step — even though we don't know what the second will be — we often get new insights and answers. Many times I charge forward without a clue of what the end of the process will be.

• *Break large projects into small steps.* The toughest part of tackling elephant-sized projects is getting started. Facing the entire task before us, we're intimidated and overwhelmed. The key is to break the project into small pieces and start with what you can do best. Doing the small job you feel most able to conquer may not be the project's logical first step, but it's the emotional first step. Getting that done encourages you to start the next most do-able step. After that, you've got momentum, and before long you're a few steps from the finish.

For example, you may see the need to develop a written statement of your church's vision and goals. Setting ten-year goals and settling on an overarching theme for your vision can't be done in a snap. But sitting down and listing needs doesn't take deep thought. Once that's out of the way, thinking about your strengths is encouraging. Then the pieces of the vision start to fall in place naturally.

● *Work in imperfect situations.* On a flight with a staff member, I opened my briefcase and started working. I noticed he read the newspaper the entire flight. I thought to myself, *We may have a problem here.* I didn't say anything about it; I wanted to see if that was an exception.

It wasn't. On the next flight he did the same thing. An hour or two into the flight, we began to discuss things to be done, and I asked him to call someone in the church. He wrote it in his calendar to do when he returned home. I asked, "Dick, when are you going to call him?"

"Well, you know, we'll be back in the office in two days," he answered. "I'll call him then."

"Dick, why don't you call him from the airport when we land," I said. "We've got an hour layover. You can handle it in five minutes."

Dick got the point quickly. He was used to working in an ideal setting, everything available and in its place.

As pastors, we wait for uninterrupted time to do our sermon preparation, and it never comes. We intend to work on the church's vision when we can get away for a few days at a cabin, but those days never become available. Looking for the perfect setting to do a task usually leads to procrastination.

I enjoy driving. There's a bit of the teenager yet in me, who loves getting into a car with some horsepower, pulling onto the expressway, and sailing down the road. When I hit the gas, my car responds because the engine is tuned, the wheels are greased, and the oil is always clean.

And that's the feeling I enjoy in ministry. After working my priorities on schedule, after paying the price, when I throttle it, I feel 400 horses under the hood.

*PART TWO*
# Getting It Done

---

*Whether you fight clutter isn't a matter of right or wrong; it's about what you want to accomplish.*

*— John Maxwell*

# CHAPTER FOUR

# Clearing the Clutter

Our church office area was designed for clutter — not the clutter of paper and files; rather, the cluttering of the pastor's schedule.

The door of the pastor's office opened into the waiting area of the administrative lobby. When the pastor exited his office, he couldn't help but see whoever was there for whatever reason. Being a people person, I would walk up, kiss the baby, and say, "How are you doing? It's good to see you. How are the kids?"

In the process I would hear an illness described or learn of something I needed to do.

Although I enjoy interacting with people like that, I found it distracted me from larger issues. It lessened my effectiveness. It was clutter.

Clutter is anything that distracts, that takes me out of focus, that keeps me from thinking or doing what I ought. Clutter is weight, baggage, whatever bogs me down.

Time wasters, for instance, are clutter. A tiff with a Sunday school teacher that preoccupies me while I pray is clutter. Thinking about my sermon while counseling is clutter. A knock at the door while I'm preparing a sermon is clutter. Trying to remember the five things I'm supposed to do today is clutter.

A pastor's life can resemble a teenager's bedroom with dirty clothes, school books, and plates strewn on the dresser, bed, floor, and desk: one-hour meetings that turn into three-hour meetings, backed up church toilets, concerns about unpaid bills, a line of Post-it notes, volunteers who don't show up, staff conflict, five-nights-a-week committee meetings, paperwork.

Under such a cascade of clutter, we may accept confusion as the norm in the local church. Or we can take positive steps to straighten up — if we really want a clean room.

## Convincing Oscar Madison

Oscar Madison, of "The Odd Couple," liked clutter, and so do many pastors. It's part of their personalities.

One of my staff members can write music, listen to a lecture, and ask a question at the same time. He thrives on having more than one thing going at once. But I'm more typical. I have to focus on one thing at a time or my work suffers. Whether you fight clutter isn't a matter of right or wrong; it's about what you want to accomplish. The less mess in my life, the more I can follow priorities, lead the church, and minister to people.

While it may not be a question of right or wrong, the more important you are in an organization, the less you can afford clutter. Effective leadership demands prioritized work, that we invest our time, gifts, and energies to fulfill a strategic vision.

Many pastors are Oscar Madisons in Felix Unger disguises. They are extremely organized yet beset with clutter, filling their schedules with things others can do. They prepare the weekly bulletin, for example, taking a day or two out of every week to write, type, cut, and paste it. That's a distraction from other priorities.

Once we decide to fight clutter, we need to recognize three kinds: schedule, emotional, administrative.

### Schedule Clutter

Interruptions clutter our days like commercials during a football game. While we can cut down on them by controlling our availability to others, such "people filters" make some pastors uncomfortable. "I'm in the people business," they say. "Being available to those in need is what ministry's all about."

I don't feel guilty about limiting people's access to me because I operate on three assumptions.

First, a pastor's job description doesn't mean being indiscriminately around others. Even Jesus limited his contact with people because of his priorities. Because he wanted to be with the Father, he went into the wilderness or up a mountain to get away from people and pray. Because he wanted to minister to Jews rather than Gentiles, when he traveled near the region of Tyre and Sidon, he ignored the request of a Gentile woman.

Was Jesus not a people person? Did he lack compassion? Of course not. Jesus limited his availability to fulfill God's special calling, which in the long run would help the most people.

If we look honestly at ourselves, we may discover that we feed on indiscriminate contact with people. It gives an excuse for avoiding other, more difficult tasks. Then we finish the day exhausted, patting ourselves on the back for having ministered to fifteen different people, half of whom did not have appointments; meanwhile sermon preparation, vision casting, or planning goes begging.

To avoid misusing time, I'm careful to protect myself and my time. When I saw how the pastor's office was set up at Skyline, with the doorway facing the main waiting area, we built a wall between the office and waiting area. That way I could walk from office to office without having to greet everyone in the lobby.

I have a second office in the attic behind our sanctuary, which provides an added level of inaccessibility. There I have most of my books and illustration files. My staff knows that I'm off-limits there except for the direst emergency. Other pastors have a second study at home or regularly use the public library or retreat centers.

A good secretary can provide help, smoothing the way for ministry while protecting leaders from clutter. If the church cannot afford a secretary to filter calls, mail, and walk-ins, a phone-answering machine will help.

Second, I minister most effectively to people if I control my availability. I need time to focus on what no one else in church can focus on: preaching, my walk with God, and leadership of the entire church.

My goal is to multiply my ministry through others. If I make myself totally available to people, I can't lead and train others effectively. Our church's ability to help people is then limited to my energy and time.

That's why I set a prioritized schedule in advance. If you don't set your schedule in advance, others will fill it for you — with no regard for your priorities. A prioritized schedule protects against interruption by providing a valid reason to say no. We can tactfully and honestly explain, "My schedule is full." On the other hand, who could say, "Your request isn't a high enough priority"?

Third, the person who wants to see me now may not have the most critical need. Consider Pastor Henry Johnson, who prepares his Sunday sermon every Friday. One week at 9:30 A.M., he begins study on a sermon on forgiveness.

At 10:30, Hilda, a church member, calls to chat. Forty-five minutes later, after cataloging her aches and pains, Hilda says good-bye.

At 11:30, Bill pops into the office. "Let's grab lunch and talk about my Sunday school class," he says. At 1:15, Pastor Johnson returns to his study.

At 1:45, the church secretary knocks on the study door and

reports, "Sorry, there's something wrong with the copy machine, and we need to get the bulletin printed." So Pastor Johnson fiddles with the machine, reads much of the copier's owner's manual, and finally at 2:30 calls a repairman.

At 3:00, the repairman arrives. The secretary has left the office early, so the pastor explains the problem to the repairman. At 3:20, he returns to his study.

At 3:50, Greg calls. "Pastor, Al asked me to mow the church grass today. Will you be there so I can get into the shed?" Fifteen minutes later Johnson walks outside with Greg to get him started.

At 4:40, Mary, a new believer, calls. "Pastor, I've been reading the Gospel of Mark, and I've got a question about . . ." Twenty minutes later, Pastor Johnson hangs up the phone and rushes out the door, late for a dinner with his new neighbors. Having barely written two pages of his sermon, he sighs, *I'll just have to write this tomorrow.*

Saturday morning, however, he receives a phone call. One of the members has had a heart attack and has been taken to a hospital an hour away. Pastor Johnson spends the entire day with the family, and that night he is too exhausted to open the books. *I'll have to get up early and do a quickie,* he decides.

Sunday morning he rushes through an hour and fifteen minutes of hurried sermon preparation and then concludes, *This one isn't going to work. I'll have to preach one out of the file.* Instead of preaching on "God Will Forgive the Worst of Sinners," he stumbles through a message on "How to Have Good Devotions."

Henry Johnson feels he's done the best he could under the circumstances: "Besides, I helped a lot of people over the weekend."

What Henry Johnson doesn't think about, though, are the number of people in his congregation — people who didn't interrupt him on Friday and Saturday — who nonetheless are in trouble: those struggling in marriage; those recently left unemployed; teenagers who are alienated from their families; seekers who are looking for meaning in life. After an ill-prepared service, such people likely walk out as they walked in: carrying the same load.

In allowing others to interrupt our schedules, we assume that whoever wants to talk to us right now has the most important need in the church. Though some of the needs pastor Johnson addressed over the weekend were critical, others were not, and as a result, some critical needs were left unmet.

With these three assumptions in mind, I can better remain a people person, and I have no qualms about controlling schedule interruptions.

People generally don't begrudge us the times we're inaccessible if we're completely available at other times. One day I was visiting with people in our church lobby when I saw Dan, our intern pastor of six months, walk in the door, briefcase in hand. On his way to his office, he strode past six people without even saying hello. Though we've set up the office to avoid indiscriminate encounters, when they happen nonetheless, I want the staff to be pastoral.

I asked to be excused from my conversation, and I followed him. "What are you doing?" I said. "You passed six people without greeting a single one."

"I'm feeling rushed," Dan responded. "I wanted to get to work."

"You just passed work when you passed people."

He worked through that over the years, and now Dan, who is now our executive pastor (and permits me to tell this story), is probably the best in our church at relationships. Fresh out of seminary, though, he thought in terms of books and paperwork; with my not-so-gentle prod, he quickly became a people person. Now he's the one I want to have handle sensitive situations, because he understands and cares deeply about people.

When we restrict our accessibility, we have to ask ourselves an important question: *Am I doing this because I want to help as many people as possible, the people God wants me to help, or because I don't want to bother with people?* If our goal is to help people, we will be readily available at other times during the week.

On Sundays my number-one priority is the people who attend. I mingle before and after the services, touching and greeting and praying with as many as I can. I stay out of my office and am in no hurry to leave after the service.

I go the extra mile to show people I care about them as individuals. I can greet 2,400 people in our church by name. I page through our directory weekly to pray for people and remember their names. We shoot a Polaroid picture of visitors, and I memorize their names so that when they walk through the door the following Sunday I can greet them by name.

I write personal notes to fifteen people every week:

"Just wanted you to know I prayed for you this week."

"Great job on that poster."

"Congratulations on John's graduation."

At church banquets I generally don't eat. I dine beforehand, assign someone else to keep our guest speaker entertained, and spend the entire time mingling.

Also, although I almost never take calls as they come, callers who do need to talk to me are told when I will return calls. Returning calls is scheduled into my day. When people learn you call as promised, they respect you and don't mind you being temporarily unavailable. It's not a sin to refuse interrupting calls, but it is not to return them.

### Emotional Clutter

What male pastor hasn't squabbled with his wife in the morning, gone to the church in a huff, and been distracted for the entire morning. He replays what he said, what she said, what he's going to say when he sees her again. Supposedly preparing a sermon — on family life, no less — he stares at the note pad for two hours but barely writes two pages.

That's emotional clutter. Feelings like anger, fear, pressure, anxiety, depression, and guilt distract us as relentlessly as the pounding bass of a teenager's stereo, making concentration and productivity impossible.

I lower the volume of emotional clutter in these ways.

● *Remember who's in charge.* It's not what happens *to* me but what happens *in* me that's critical. I'm the one who decides how I will respond to any situation.

Long ago I realized right thinking didn't eliminate difficult times. In fact, positive thinkers have as many problems as do negative thinkers. The difference? Negative thinkers react wrongly and therefore compound their problems. Positive thinkers respond correctly and therefore conquer their problems.

• *Deal aggressively with overcommitments.* Stress does more than make us nervous; it pumps steam into all our emotions, heightening their intensity, distracting us even more from our focus. Instead of getting only a little irritated over a volunteer who drops the ball, we're furious. Instead of being only slightly let down by low attendance on a Sunday, we descend into deep depression and consider resigning.

So one key to handling emotional clutter is to guard against the stress that comes from overcommitment. Here are five ways I turn down that heat.

1. Delegate tasks. I tend to believe I can always do more, that a job needs less of my time than it actually does. When I've overcommitted myself, the first thing I do is delegate.

That was possible even before I had a staff. In my first church I had no staff. My method was to spend as much time with people as possible, visiting, praying, meeting needs, making new acquaintances.

As the church grew, I did much of the office work myself, typing, filing, paying bills. Eventually I was stretched too thin. Since we couldn't afford a secretary, I asked members to answer the phone and take messages. Before long they picked up other office work. It wasn't a perfect arrangement, but it relieved some of the pressure.

2. Regain your perspective. When I'm feeling the pressure that everything depends on me, I'm taking myself too seriously. I need to back off.

When you're in a rut, the answer is not to shovel more furiously; it's to get out of the hole, to gain perspective. *Why am I doing this? Maybe I shouldn't even be shoveling that hole. Will it help to keep doing more of the same? Should I be digging somewhere else?*

My wife, Margaret, is my best friend. Often she helps me gain a balanced perspective about my life and family. Occasionally we have "one of those talks" where she helps me step back and see where my life is headed. When I listen without defensiveness, I often see my error and begin to make needed adjustments. With proper perspective, I make sound decisions on how to shuffle priorities.

3. Jettison unnecessary commitments. If I can't delegate my overcommitments, as a last resort and as much as I hate to, I occasionally ask out of an obligation.

I once canceled a commitment to address a conference in New Zealand. It was a painful decision, but I had been asking my family to sacrifice time with me for too long, and enough was enough. They needed to spend more time with me, and my schedule had no openings in sight.

4. Prevent overcommitments on the front end. I now have an evaluation committee comprised of my wife, my administrative assistant, and a couple of other trusted individuals. The committee reviews all speaking invitations and decides which I can accept. They help me see things more objectively and allow me to say no to people I'd have a hard time turning down.

5. Accept tradeoffs. Our church is about to begin a huge fund drive, and so for the next three months I will have to be at my best. The church cannot be distracted, and all plans and programs have to be well-prepared. So I'll need to be in church every Sunday to have things running like clockwork.

I've discussed this with my family, and they understand that for the next few months they'll see less of me than they'd like. But I promised to make up for it: "Over the Christmas holiday we're going to take a special vacation, a trip to Hawaii."

Obviously this was an exceptional tradeoff, but we can always make it up to whomever is paying an extra price for our busyness. When we do promise a tradeoff, we have to follow through. "Honey, something else has come up," will be the end of us.

● *Pursue intimacy with God and spouse.* Emotional clutter results when the deepest need of our hearts — closeness, intimacy —goes unmet. That can lead to disaster

There are lots of substitutes. Instead of finding satisfaction in being close to God, we may pursue success. If we don't succeed, we become angry and frustrated.

Or we may try to find meaning in needing to be needed — codependency. We run ourselves into the ground trying to please everyone. We end up angry, depressed, and anxious.

If we lack intimacy with our spouses, we may try to find it in other relationships, sometimes ending up in sexual sin or pornography, awash in guilt. Efforts to fill the void in our hearts outside of intimacy with God and family make us emotionally vulnerable.

Now and then I tell my congregation, "I love you with all my heart and am committed to serving you. But my love for you can't compare with the love I feel for my Lord, my wife, and my kids. They are the highest joys in my life. Ministry is gravy."

### Administrative Clutter

Administrative clutter includes paperwork, work done by you that should be done by others, and snarls in communication or the chain of authority.

Administrative clutter seems to come from everyone and everything around us, like debris carried by swirling flood waters. But its real fountainhead is within, springing from the needs, fears, and desires of the leader. Here are some essentials for straightening up administrative clutter.

● *Release the need to control everything.* Someone asked me once, "Are you still running the church?"

"No, I haven't run the church for about five years," I answered. "I'm leading it, but I have a lot of people running it."

The greater our need to control every decision, practice, program, and activity of our church, the more nonessential matters will consume our time and energies.

For example, while I need to train those who work around me, I also must let them work in the way they find best. Recently I've hired a new personal assistant. She's a competent administrator who organizes her schedule and mine with a different system than the one used by my previous assistant — an extremely competent woman as well. But I don't care how she organizes the details as long as we get as much done, and done as well. As long as people hit the ball, I don't worry how they swing the bat.

At Skyline, at least ten people know more about what's happening in the church than I do. I have confidence in them, and I've released control. I have no qualms about giving them credit for what's getting done.

We've made light-handed leadership our church policy. At Skyline, decision making and problem solving are done at the lowest possible levels, by the staff members, committee members, or leaders directly working with ministries. The board doesn't decide whether or not the church should buy a new typewriter! The only matters that come to me or the board are those only we are qualified to handle. (We even canceled one board meeting this year because we didn't have enough to talk about.)

● *Overcome the need to be needed.* When our need to be needed gets out of hand, we attract clutter like an electromagnet attracts scrap iron. As pastors, we like being the information hub of the church. We feel important when time and again we're asked, "Pastor, what should we do about . . . ?" It's draining, but we like it. Having to know all, though, fills our ministries with clutter.

I do several things to repel information clutter. I've told my staff and leaders that while there are some things I always want to know — the mood of the church, relationship problems among staff or leaders, decisions that aren't working — I don't need or want to know everything.

For example, my assistant meets for lunch regularly with various leaders in the church, and she returns with a list of ten or so things that are happening in their areas. I've told her, "Select the two or three most important points on the list. That's all I can remember or do anything about anyway."

In other settings I handle information in one of four ways:

1. Don't receive it. People in your church learn what information "turns your crank." If someone passes "scrap iron" to me —

for example, minor conflict among workers in one of the depart-
ments or criticism of a staff member's program — I'll dryly say,
"Okay; thanks," and that's all. I won't dismiss it arrogantly, but
people get the message.

2. *Receive information with someone who can manage it.*
When I attend a meeting where there's a possibility I'll walk away
with something to do, I bring my assistant. I can delegate the work
to her on the spot without having to explain the context of what
needs doing, as I would if I left her at the office.

This can be done with lay people, but we have to get comfortable
bringing others into the process. A secretive, play-things-close-to-the-
vest approach to ministry insures that your vest pockets will be full of
clutter.

3. *Receive information after someone has worked on it.* When
we need to process information into a message, article, or report, or
when we need to research a subject, we have a choice between two
leadership styles. We can do the spadework ourselves and then
hand it to another for reaction, editing, and improvement. Or we
can have someone research and put together the information, and
then we review, edit, and refocus as needed.

My preference is the latter. After someone else does the first
80 percent of the thinking, I add my 20 percent. After my assistant
carries the ball as far as she can, I take it the rest of the way.

4. *Receive it and immediately do something about it.* My goal
here is to plug information into a calendar, file, or box so I don't
have to bother remembering it. Anything to remember is clutter.

When I go to denominational conferences, for instance, in my
briefcase I have files labeled for the information I'll receive or produce — one file for my assistant, another for our executive pastor,
another still for sermon outlines and illustrations. As I think of
things to do or receive printed material or write messages, they
immediately go into the appropriate file. That way I can forget about
them, and when I get home, I just hand out files.

● *Release jobs that are enjoyable but not essential.* I used to keep
track of the numbers at church: offerings, attendance, baptisms,
conversions. I would spend an hour each week compiling records,

as gleeful as a toy maker at Christmas, thanking God for progress, envisioning new goals.

At my second church one day, I was seated at my desk with ushers' reports and financial reports spread out before me. Suddenly I realized, *This is ridiculous! I'm spending my time with an adding machine and graphs when someone else could do this and give me the results.* So I sheepishly got out of my chair, walked out of my office, and said to my secretary, "Give me fifty minutes, and I'll show you what I'd like you to do for me."

At the time, that was one of the hardest things for me to let go of, but it was unnecessary clutter. Obviously we need some emotional rewards in our work, and I could have kept doing it for the sake of enjoyment, but I chose to release it to devote my energies to "new and better toys."

● *Overcome the fear of a subordinate's failure.* If you can't bear a job done wrong or risk the failure of subordinates, the work piles will litter not their desks but yours.

When our executive pastor hired his first employee, he quickly discovered he chose the wrong person. But I couldn't fault him, because when I look in the mirror I see someone who makes mistakes every day. So we sat down and discussed how to prevent a repeat performance.

I have an understanding with subordinates. They have the freedom to make mistakes as long as they allow me the freedom to step in and use those mistakes as teaching opportunities. I take time weekly to sit down with my executive pastor and discuss wins and losses.

Delegating clutter is never enough. Without adequately training workers, we actually increase snarls. For example, when others seek help and your subordinate can't solve their problems adequately, people lose confidence in your subordinate and quickly learn to bypass him or her and come straight to you. My aim: to recruit the right people and train them until they inspire confidence, until others would rather deal with them than me!

God is creatively at work in his church. But the pastorate, like virgin wilderness, can be a tangle, cluttered by trees, underbrush, and rocks.

These acres don't change from wilderness to productive farmland without brush clearing, rock collecting, and sod busting. Ministry doesn't become a place of order and fruitfulness without clutter clearing.

*Others may assign us tasks and make demands on us, but we control our own time.*

*— Steven McKinley*

CHAPTER FIVE
# Time Bandits

---

Everybody wastes some time. And everybody thinks wasting time is a bad thing. But what is *wasted time*?

In their book *Manage Your Time, Manage Your Work, Manage Yourself*, Merrill E. Douglass and Donna N. Douglass say, "You waste your time whenever you spend it on something less important when you could be spending it on something more important. Importance is determined by measuring your activities against your objectives."

When we measure the way we actually spend our time with

our objectives, it usually becomes clear that we *are* wasting time. We just don't get done everything we expect, reasonably so, to get done in a week. When that happens week after week, that's frustrating.

So how does one go about trimming wasted time?

I start with this assumption: we are in control of our own time. No one else controls it for us. Others may assign us tasks and make demands on us, but we control our own time. I'm not aware of any pastors who punch time clocks or who work under supervisors who rigidly order their days. Instead, we pastors have a great deal of freedom to structure our own time.

That means other people cannot waste our time for us. We waste our own time, sometimes by handing it over to others to spend (or waste) however they please! Getting control of our waste time means getting control of ourselves.

In this chapter, we will look at some of the time-wasters that torment pastors, and some ways I deal with those time-wasters.

## Disorganization

My friend Jim is one of the most harried people I know. He often complains about his heavy work load and his inability to keep up with others' demands.

Recently I visited with Jim in his office and learned why he's so harried. His office was a large junk closet. His desk was stacked with papers, files, old bulletins, empty coffee cups, non-functioning pens, and little scraps of yellow paper with notes written on them. His attaché case overflowed with paper. Years of magazines were piled on the credenza.

At Jim's invitation, I cleared a few hymnals off a chair and sat down. As we talked, we got around to the annual statistical report then due at denominational headquarters. Jim started hunting for his copy. "I know it's on this desk somewhere," he said.

As he sorted through the papers, he found a letter concerning a community meeting he had planned to attend the previous week but had forgotten about. He uncovered an envelope containing a $100 check for the building fund. He located several bills now overdue and collecting interest. Finally he found the statistical report.

"I don't know how they expect a person to do all this," Jim said with disgust. "I don't even have enough time to get organized."

Even Jim knows what his problem is. He's so disorganized everything takes him longer than it should. But he doesn't know how to get organized, and he claims he doesn't have the time to get organized.

The title of a book by the noted time-management expert Jeffrey J. Mayer puts the question pointedly: *If You Haven't Got the Time to Do It Right, When Will You Find the Time to Do It Over?* That title suggests that when we take time now to get organized, we save time ahead! Time-honored principles, like handling each piece of paper only once and making good use of files, are time-honored because they work. If Jim would take time to clear his desk and keep it clear, use an appointment book, develop a filing system, and keep records of pastoral work, he would see a many-fold return on time invested.

### Chasing Rabbits

I remember the first time I tried to walk to the neighborhood store with our dog, Peewee. We called him Peewee as a joke, for he was a big, lumbering brute of no certain breed. I was just a tadpole. When I took the leash, I thought I would be in charge of this walk.

I wasn't. As we walked the few blocks to the market, Peewee kept seeing rabbits and chasing them, dragging me down alleys and across yards. Finally I gave up and encouraged Peewee to drag me home. We never did make it to the market.

Some days I catch myself working the way Peewee walked to the market. I head in one direction, then I get distracted. I chase one rabbit after another and never get around to what I intended in the first place.

I pull out the denominational directory to look up an address and notice my old buddy Ken has moved to a new congregation. Then I wonder who is pastor now at Ken's old congregation, so I look it up. And since Ken and I were neighbors in another state, I take time to see who is pastoring in that area now, and how they're doing, as far as statistics are concerned.

But just thinking about Ken and his new call can set me to fantasizing. Ken took a call to a congregation in the Sun Belt. What would that be like? I look up a few congregations in the Sun Belt, just to get some idea of their size, finances.

By the time I get around to looking up the address I started out after, I've wasted a lot of time chasing rabbits.

I chase other kinds of rabbits now and then. I go to the bookcase for a commentary and wind up rearranging the biblical studies section. I go to the files for a copy of the church blueprints for the property committee and stand at the filing cabinet reading the minutes of the last building committee. I call the church treasurer about a bill and get so involved talking about our golf games that I never get around to that bill.

To avoid wasting time, I seek to focus on the job at hand and ignore the rabbits, no matter how tempting.

**Perfectionism**

It was 4:30 on a Friday afternoon, often a low time of the week for me. I was going to read through my sermon one more time, review the bulletin for Sunday morning, and then go home.

But when I read through the bulletin, I discovered a terrible mistake. We were honoring our Sunday school teachers that Sunday. Their names were printed in the bulletin, but somehow our secretary had missed the name of Muriel Erickson, the long-time teacher of the third-grade class.

This was a mistake I couldn't tolerate. But my secretary was gone for the day, and I knew she had plans to be out of town on Saturday. There was only one thing left to do: redo the bulletin myself.

I called my wife to tell her I would be late for dinner that night. "The bulletin is all wrong," I said. "I have to stay and do it over again."

I was wrong on two counts. First, the bulletin was not "all wrong." There was one mistake. Second, I didn't *have to* redo it. I chose to, and that was a waste of time. I could have called Muriel. She would have understood. But that went against my grain.

I fight continually against the disease of perfectionism. Unless absolutely everything is exactly right, it isn't good enough, as far as I'm concerned, and it's my responsibility to make everything right, no matter how long it takes.

But I end up feeling burdened and depressed about how much time I'm putting into trying to achieve perfection.

A doctor told a friend of mine that for $100 of tests, he could give my friend Howard a 75 percent assurance he was in good health. For another $200, he could give an 85 percent assurance. For $200 beyond that, he could give a 95 percent assurance. For another $200 beyond that (now we're up to $700), he could give Howard a 98 percent assurance of his good health.

Howard decided on $100 in tests, to get the 75 percent assurance and stop at that. For him, the cost of greater assurance outweighed the benefits.

I try to apply that to pastoral work, asking myself, *When is it no longer worth my time to struggle toward perfection?*

Take preaching, for example. While I envision sermons and select themes weeks and months in advance, I can usually write my sermon in about four hours. This usually produces a sermon that faithfully proclaims God's Word and touches people who hear it.

If I were to study six, eight, or ten hours, I could make it a better sermon. I might be very proud of it. My old preaching professors might think well of me. Perhaps I could get it published in a magazine. But would it have a measurably greater impact on hearers? Probably not.

While there is nothing wrong with the pursuit of excellence, while I do struggle mightily to produce the best sermon I can every week, it is not necessarily a good use of my time to spend ten hours every week trying to produce a perfect sermon. It is a waste of time, first, because there are more important ways I could use the extra six hours. Second, it is a waste of time because (here's the hard one) *perfection is beyond my grasp.* No matter how much time I put into my sermon, there are still some who "don't get it," some who don't like it, and some who don't care enough to pay much attention to it.

We proclaim the good news of a God who loves us as we are, who embraces imperfect people. It is inconsistent at best and theologically flawed at worst for us to live as though those standards do not apply to us, as though our work must be perfect or it is unacceptable. The gospel tells me to labor mightily to do my best without ever deluding myself about achieving perfection.

### Poor Use of Secretary

Proverbs 31 extols the virtues of the "capable wife . . . worth far more than jewels" (TEV). As far as I'm concerned, the author could have been describing church secretaries.

Not every pastor is fortunate enough to have a secretary. I not only have a secretary, I have an excellent secretary who saves me hours daily. She is a great "people person," who deals with callers and visitors tactfully, cheerfully, and firmly. She knows me well enough to know what calls I *want* to take and what people I *want* to see, and she has a sharp enough ministry sense to know what calls I *should* take and what people I *should* see.

My secretary saves time by protecting me from salespeople eager to sell us a new telephone system, from requests to inventory the coffee or the coffee cups, from people who just want to chat, from traveling evangelists looking for a place to plant themselves for a night or two. On particularly busy days, she encourages me to close my door so I can concentrate. She takes initiative to order needed supplies, keeps meticulous files, oversees the congregation's master calendar, and placates some of the disgruntled.

Those who can't afford a secretary should make every effort to recruit volunteers. Any time they can give is better than nothing. And pastors who have secretaries should spare no expense in providing them training through seminars, books, and newsletters. When you invest in a secretary's skills, you're buying time!

### Not Calling Ahead

Sometimes I'm ready to curse Alexander Graham Bell. His telephone on the corner of my desk is said to be a great invention, but some days it interrupts so incessantly I want to toss it out the window. While some of my colleagues now have cellular car phones, a telephone in my office is more than enough for me!

At the same time, I remind myself, *The telephone is your friend.* I can think of an afternoon recently when I should have made better use of my friend than I did.

I had left the office after lunch to make a hospital call thirty minutes away. At the hospital, I discovered my parishioner had been discharged the day before.

On my way back to church, I reached into my pocket for the visitor cards from the previous Sunday. I picked out the card of one family, located their address in a new development, and marched up to the door. No one home.

Frustrated but determined to make a call that afternoon, I headed for a senior citizens' apartment complex, home to one of our shut-ins. I discovered she was visiting with friends from her old neighborhood. She insisted on serving me cake and coffee, but my visit with her was not what I had hoped. By the time I headed back to the office, I had wasted most of the afternoon.

I could have avoided that by following one simple rule: phone first. In contemporary culture, that's even more important. Hospital stays are much shorter than they once were. Most adults work outside the home. Even shut-ins can be busy people.

Even if our unannounced visits catch prospects at home, we're better off calling ahead. In our culture today, old-fashioned drop-in calls simply do not work. People are so busy they don't welcome drop-in callers any more than pastors enjoy people dropping in at church to chat.

A double-barreled approach to eliminating wasted time: I have my secretary do the calling for me.

### Not Setting Limits

In my early months at this congregation, Jean stormed in one day. She looped around my secretary, came to my door, and asked, "Pastor, do you have a few minutes?"

I was preparing for a church council, but eager to be a "good pastor." I said, "Certainly I do," came from behind my desk to the coffee table and chairs, poured two cups of coffee, and sat down.

Jean took off on the fly, telling me all her problems: an alcoholic husband, alienated adult children, conflicts with my predecessor, ill health, inability to keep a job.

I practiced my best listening and counseling skills, but my observations and suggestions were rejected. I tried to steer the conversation, to zero in on specific complaints, but Jean defied steering.

The "few minutes" I had promised ballooned into three hours. Then she marched out of the office as suddenly as she had come.

After several more similar visits with Jean, I decided to set some limits. It's important to meet the needs of individuals as I'm able, but it's wrong for me to abandon my responsibility to the entire congregation to serve one individual. When we leave our time at the mercy of others, we give people permission to waste our time. I've learned always to be available, in a limited way.

Now when Jean comes to my office — and she still does — with her standard question "Do you have a few minutes?" I tell her I have one hour. In that hour I am fully and intently "with" Jean. At the end of the hour, I say, "Jean, I have another commitment." (True: a commitment to the rest of my ministry!)

Counselors say the last ten minutes of counseling sessions are usually the most productive. That's when deep hurts come out, when the real issues are dealt with. Whether you give a counselee one hour or three hours, you still get most of "their stuff" the last ten minutes.

I also set limits on telephone time. Every congregation has telephone tyrants who keep us on the phone excessively as they wander from one subject to another. My goal on the telephone is to discuss what's necessary and then get off. When I call someone else, I try to have my purpose clearly in mind, and when ending the conversation, even telephone tyrants understand when I simply say, "I've got to go now." I'm under no obligation to say *why*.

Small talk is necessary — it's the mortar of relationships —

but it can be overdone. Protracted conversations about the weather and the fate of local athletic teams eats up too much time if we let it. In Minnesota, it will be cold in January, and we can be relatively sure the Vikings will not win the Super Bowl.

## Reading Useless Mail

They say we form lifetime habits when we are children. As a boy, I would watch for the mailman. I could see him zig-zag his way down the street and then walk up the steps to our front porch. As he walked away, I ran out the front door and grabbed the mail. Of course mail rarely came for me, but when it did, I would tear into it.

So conditioned, it's hard for me to throw away mail unopened. But some mail that crosses my desk deserves discarding. When the return address is a stained-glass company, I toss it. We don't have any stained glass in our building, and I know that in my lifetime we won't.

Our building is fairly new, so I don't need to read the latest mailing from the sandblasting and tuck-pointing company.

I know some publishers don't produce material we can use in our Sunday school, so I toss their advertisements.

And those little plastic packages of advertising cards we all receive head straight for the wastebasket.

Conquering the mail addiction, which insists we read every piece that crosses our desk, will add minutes to each day, minutes that add up to hours.

## When Waste Is Not

While I work hard to manage my time, I do allow myself to waste time here and there.

Our church runs a daycare center. Our building is fairly compact, so I see our "daycare kids" many times daily.

Mark was not one of the easiest students ever to attend our daycare. He was loud and demanding, high-strung and aggressive. Every time I saw him, he wanted to show me the picture he was working on, or tell me about the television program he watched the night before, or report on the latest shenanigans of the other kids.

He had a way about him that demanded attention, so I would usually stop and talk with him, even when I felt pressed by other responsibilities. Sometimes our conversations went on and on, and my frustration would rise. I've never been good at disappointing kids, so I played along, allowing myself to "waste" time on Mark.

A few months ago, Mark's single mother, who had little church background, started attending our church. She has since joined, started working out some significant personal problems, and is getting involved.

I recently asked her why she started attending. "Mark wanted to come," she said. "He told me, 'Most people don't like me, but Pastor McKinley always listens to me.' " The painful insight of a 5 year old.

"I'm glad you do," his mother continued. "Thank you."

*One of the best ways to show I care about others is to manage my time well.*

— *John Maxwell*

CHAPTER SIX
# Put Time
# on Your Side

---

Samuel Plimsoll, a member of the English Parliament in the 1800s, crusaded for the safety of merchant seamen. To outlaw what Plimsoll called "coffin ships," overloaded and therefore unseaworthy vessels often heavily insured by their unscrupulous owners, Parliament enacted the Merchant Shipping Act of 1876.

This act required all merchant ships to have a load line, a line on the hull that would be visible above the water if a ship was carrying a safe weight. An overloaded ship would submerge the line. This load line came to be known as the Plimsoll mark.

Sometimes pastors need a "Plimsoll mark." I remember all too well a time when mine would have been six feet under water.

I had committed myself to speak at leadership conferences six weeks in a row — in addition to pastoring my church. When those six weeks were over, I had spoken 72 times and traveled over 18,000 miles without a single day off. I felt awful.

When I see an opportunity, I tend to go after it, assuming I can somehow find time for it. Most pastors, I believe, are similarly tempted. The lure may be speaking engagements, counseling appointments, or community involvement.

Of course, I didn't overcommit myself in one fell stroke. I agreed to speak at a few conferences, then a few more opportunities came my way, then a few more still. Suddenly in one of my brighter moments, I realized I was foundering.

That was about four years ago. The good ship Maxwell didn't sink, but I think I'm smarter now. For one thing, as I've mentioned earlier, I formed an evaluation committee comprised of my wife, my office assistant, and two friends; they decide what commitments I can accept, and they tend to veto most of the invitations I receive.

In addition to my evaluation committee, here are nine other ways I keep my Plimsoll mark safely above the water line.

**Let Your Secretary Manage Your Calendar**

Most pastors hesitate to relinquish control of their calenders to their secretaries, fearing they'll also turn over control of their lives. When they feel energized to write the sermon, the schedule will demand they counsel.

To prevent that, I give my assistant clear parameters and explain my scheduling preferences.

For example, I've told her to schedule my appointments back-to-back, without even five minutes between them. Years ago I found I couldn't get anything substantial done during five- to thirty-minute gaps. All I did was shuffle papers and wait.

I also give my input into the calendar early. I'll tell my assistant I've got nine projects for the next month, and I want a half-day for each. Sometimes I'll specify which days.

By turning over my calendar to another, what I lose in flexibility, I gain in time. First, I save the time it takes arranging appointments. My assistant handles all the calls. When problems arise, say a canceled appointment, my assistant is free to make adjustments. She might move a later appointment to the earlier slot or add thirty minutes to my sermon preparation block.

Second, I avoid the temptation to waste time. If I control my schedule, I'm more likely to follow my feelings than my priorities. If I'm tired and an appointment is canceled, for example, I might just dawdle over a magazine.

### Do More Pitching than Fielding

Are you a fielder or a pitcher? Fielders react to where the ball is hit. Pitchers control the ball.

Most congregations think of pastors as fielders chasing the action. If we let them, people ring the phone all day, every day and determine the course of our week:

"I need you to make a hospital visit to someone my mother works with."

"We would like you to come to our Sunday school social."

We may assume people have the right to dictate our schedules, and we may feel guilty if we don't "take care of the flock." But I think that's false guilt. The first thing I do is block out the hours I need to work on my sermons and other ministry responsibilities, and then, remembering that even pitchers have to field their position, I deal with the ministry opportunities that others bring to me.

### Screen Calls

Screening calls doesn't just mean having a secretary answer the phone. Receptionists/secretaries can save us time only if they're trained to deal with callers.

I recently talked to a receptionist who, after informing me that the party I was seeking was not in, asked if she could help. I told her what I was after, and she gave me all I needed. "Tell your boss he doesn't need to return the call," I said before hanging up.

This receptionist asked questions, and that's the first thing I train our receptionists to do. Half the callers who want me can be better helped by another staff person. If the caller is unfamiliar to the receptionist, the first question is "Can I tell Pastor Maxwell the purpose of your call?" or "Can I or someone else in the church help you?"

I have given these screeners a list of people with whom I always want to talk, no questions asked, as well as the small number of people who can interrupt me as necessary. I tell my assistant what my priorities are so that she can use her judgment about who to put through. Some callers don't want to tell my assistant the purpose of their call. So I've instructed her to say, "Pastor is not available now. If he knows the purpose of your call, he may be able to give me the answer to pass along, or he can be better prepared when he calls you back."

### Work in a Work Environment

Some places have more distractions and opportunities to waste time than others. Some pastors think that is home. But I've found that two kinds of people work at home. The lazy and the productive.

Most people don't get as much work done at home as they could at the office. They're tempted to sleep in, eat a late breakfast, read the paper, watch "Donahue." Already having too little structure in their days, many pastors need more of the mindset of a blue-collar worker: punch in and punch out. Working in the office provides this.

Then again, hard workers often have their office at home. They work no matter where they are, but at home they get more done because they avoid office distractions.

I've worked out a compromise. As I mentioned previously, I have a separate office in the church, tucked away in a far, upstairs corner of the facilities. When I go there, my assistant knows I'm not to be disturbed, and that's where I usually work on my sermons.

## Delegate

Delegation is a mixed blessing.

I once heard it put this way: "An executive has practically nothing to do except to decide what is to be done; to tell somebody to do it; to listen to reasons why it should not be done, why it should be done by someone else, or why it should be done in a different way; to follow up to see if the thing has been done; to discover that it has not; to inquire why; to listen to excuses from the person who should have done it; to follow up again to see if the thing has been done, only to discover that it has been done incorrectly; to point out how it should have been done; to conclude that as long as it has been done, it may as well be left where it is; to wonder if it is not time to get rid of a person who cannot do a thing right; to reflect that he probably has a wife and large family, and that certainly any successor would be just as bad, or maybe worse; to consider how much simpler and better the thing would have been done if one had done it oneself in the first place; to reflect sadly that one could have done it right in twenty minutes, and, as things turned out, one has had to spend two days to find out why it has taken three weeks for somebody else to do it wrong."

But some of the most productive people in history have found that delegation is more than frustration. "I owe whatever success I have attained," said Andrew Carnegie, "by and large to my ability to surround myself with people who are smarter than I am."

Delegation is an opportunity. After others get training and experience, they may be more gifted than we are at their ministries. And although it initially takes more time to give work to others, in the long run we save time.

That only happens, however, if we delegate rather than dump. We dump work on others when we give jobs on the spur of the moment; if we fail to take into account others' unique gifts, personalities, and interests; if we don't provide coaching, preparation, and information; if we give out jobs because we're frustrated rather than because we have the right jobs for the right people. Dumping always causes more problems than it solves.

All I did in my early ministry was dump. I didn't understand the value or discipline of delegating, and I certainly didn't know how to do it. I would try to do everything myself, and when I ran out of time and a job was undone, I would dump. As time went on I discovered that delegating is equipping. That changed my approach to assigning responsibilities.

Successful delegation has the following characteristics:

● *Know yourself.* This rule governs all the points. One person does not have the gifts or time to do everything.

One of the greatest things you discover is your strengths and gifts. I know what jobs are required of me by the church, what jobs I get the greatest return doing, and what jobs give me a personal sense of reward. All other jobs I try to delegate.

● *Know your team.* "Don't put a sword in a madman's hand," says one English proverb. That's a strong way of saying that the wrong people can do a lot of harm both to themselves and others (and me!). So however great the need, I don't give a ministry to others unless I think they're suited.

● *Clearly define the task.* This doesn't mean always telling someone how to do a job. If people are capable, often it is better to allow them to figure out how to do a job in the way that best suits them. But I must tell workers what results I'm looking for and what I expect of them.

● *Provide the resources necessary to accomplish the task.* That may include a budget, facilities, training seminars, curriculum, promotion.

● *Encourage feedback.* One sure way to make a person feel abandoned is to fail to communicate. After a person begins a job, there will always be questions, problems, refinements. I want to help people learn, and on-the-job training is the most effective way. I like to ask the questions: How are you progressing? Any problems? Anything I can do to help?

● *Clarify the level of authority given.* How free are people to make decisions and take action? Are they to (1) report a situation to you so that you make all decisions, (2) make recommendations about their work though you still decide, (3) choose a course of action but wait for approval, (4) deal with situations but advise you of what they did, or (5) handle their responsibilities without advising you of their actions?

● *Hold people accountable.* I try to keep in mind a rule of accountability I read some time ago: when I delegate authority to act, I don't abdicate my responsibility to get the job done. If the people to whom I delegate responsibility fail, that, in the end, is the consequence of my leadership — it has failed in that instance. So that reminds me that I have the responsibility to hold people accountable.

● *Recognize effort and reward results.* I want to make people glad they have been working for me. So I tell people when they've done good work, and I like to make that known publicly, from the pulpit or through the church newsletter.

When I follow these guidelines, I delegate successfully, and the person to whom I've delegated wins, the church wins, and I win. My mind has been freed up, as has my schedule for other, needful tasks.

As I learned to delegate, though, I had to free myself from the need to know everything going on in the church; I can't when I effectively delegate. In San Diego we have a radio personality on KFMB who calls himself "Mr. Answerman." People call in with questions — about anything — and he answers (though sometimes he makes things up). I now pride myself in not having a clue about many things going on in our church, though I do want to know where a person can get the answer. That shows me that I've been delegating.

### Get Started

There's a sermon to write. Now on Friday afternoon, you have a five-hour "window" to get it done, adequate time to work without pressure. But you haven't had a chance this week to pray and think at length about what to preach on. Last night you slept poorly, and now you have a dull headache and no energy.

You sharpen your pencils. You cut your fingernails. You make a pot of coffee, glance through *Newsweek*, jot down announcements for Sunday, clear off your desk, reread some of the ads from yesterday's mail, daydream about your son's ballgame tonight. Now your time window has shrunk to just over four hours.

Slowly getting around to work decreases the amount of time you have for the project, putting time pressure on that and other jobs, increasing the feeling that you're being swamped by higher and higher waves of work.

On the other hand, training ourselves to dive into work when the gun sounds, without asking whether we want to or whether we feel like it, sooner or later energizes us.

Harvard psychologist Jerome Brunner says, "You're more likely to act yourself into a feeling than to feel yourself into action."

I've found it's best to sit with a pad of paper and jot ideas down for Sunday's sermon whether I feel inspired or not. I don't wait for an emotional high to get started; the high comes when the work is done.

### Do Two Things at Once

Some obligations require large blocks of our time but don't require our full attention.

I recently traveled to Des Moines for our denomination's general convention. Since most of the business didn't involve me, it could have been a major waste of time.

So I did double duty. During the sessions I looked through books and magazines and trolled for sermon ideas and illustrations. I kept a legal pad handy and brainstormed ideas for our fall stewardship campaign. I wrote lists of things to do when I returned home.

Whenever I needed to get my mind into the meeting, I did. I even helped support a couple of pieces of legislation.

### Get Organized

Hunting for what's lost is the number one thief of time.

Preachers have opportunities for major hunting expeditions every week. You're writing Sunday's sermon and remember an illustration that will make the sermon a four-star message. *I read that in a book a couple of months ago. Now which one was it?* You hurry to the bookshelf, choose a likely candidate, and start reading.

Twenty-five minutes later, still not finding the story, you decide, *I must not have underlined it.* So you skim each chapter. Thirty minutes later you realize, *It isn't in this book. I must have read the story in that new book of illustrations.* You pull out the illustration book and wonder, *Now, how would they index that story? Under "love," "discipline," "parenting"?* An hour later, after searching two other books and one magazine, you find the prized illustration.

Shelves of books, boxes of magazines, and unorganized files of clippings can bury preachers like a tidal wave. I learned early that I had to have a retrieval system. I began as a teenager, writing quotes on index cards. I now have staff people who spend hours each week filing materials for me.

I "fish" more than I read. I rarely finish a magazine article. Rather, I read titles and callouts and blurbs to see if an article may be useful. If so, I read the introduction and see what the major principles are. Once I determine the payoff of the article, I either move on or rip it out, write what subject I want it filed under, and put it in a file for my secretary.

I'm not in love with books. They're only a means to an end for me. I bracket quotes and illustrations. In the white pages I'll write "Page 37 — Faith." When I finish the book, I hand it to my assistant, who copies and files the excerpts. The book is gutted; I don't need it anymore; I can give it away.

We can also waste our time handling, rehandling, and hunting in "pile files" for correspondence. Never read a letter twice. Have a system in place so that you put a letter where it belongs the first time you handle it, either in an out box for someone else, in a storage, or work, or "tickler" file (a dated file that contains work that doesn't need to be addressed until the date), or in the trash.

## Work in the Car

My car is an office. I easily spend an hour a day in my car, so I have it equipped with a car phone, a microcassette recorder (for dictating), a note pad, and a tape player. In my car are usually forty cassettes from various tape clubs for pastors, *Preaching Today*,

*Pastor's Update,* and my own *Injoy.* I can cross the country and not run out of tapes.

On my way home from the office I'll typically return four or five phone calls, pray with people over the phone, and call others just to say I appreciate what they're doing.

## Keep Time Management in Perspective

If I'm too busy to treat people with kindness, I need to get out of the people business or lighten up my schedule. But for me it really isn't a choice between time management or taking time for people. By making the most of my time, I'm able to show thoughtfulness in ways others may feel their schedule doesn't allow. ·

I send a lot of personal notes. I keep cards in my briefcase so I can write notes to people while I'm on a plane or sitting at a stoplight: "It was great talking to you today. I want you to know I appreciate you and enjoyed our few minutes together."

We have communication cards in the pews for people to tell the staff their prayer requests. Every week these requests fill seven pages, single-spaced. Each week I'll go through the list and pray for each person. I can't contact everyone personally, but I do try to make contact with those who are facing really tough times. I will call and pray with some people over the phone and send notes to others.

These are just some of the ways my schedule allows me to care for people individually. In the meantime, I've led a ministry where people are cared for by programs and staff and hundreds of lay volunteers.

I've found, then, that one of the best ways to show I care about others is to manage my time well.

*Unless the hours in a week are harnessed meaningfully, they become a wasted natural resource. Time waits for no one; time returns for no one.*

— *Greg Asimakoupoulos*

# The Workweek

---

Did you know that an American president spent as much time in his White House bedroom as he spent in the Oval Office? His name was Calvin Coolidge. History reports that on average Coolidge slept eleven hours each night.

Compare that with this extreme opposite: the president of a seminary I attended averaged only four hours of sleep each night. Apparently that was the only way he could juggle lecturing, publishing, administrating, and keeping up with an extensive speaking schedule.

We are each different. Our internal clocks and personal preferences determine, to a large extent, the way we order our days and nights. After a full Sunday of preaching and pastoral care, for example, many pastors routinely take Mondays off. For them it is an absolute necessity to recharge their emotional batteries for the week to come.

Other pastors, however, work Mondays. They insist that the day-after depression often following Sunday should not ruin a perfectly good day off. Rather they choose to feel lousy at church, spending Mondays dealing with administration. Later in the week, when they are brimming with energy, these pastors take a day off.

Who's to say which is right?

The same is true of pastors organizing their weeks. Every pastor, every method, is different. Some plans are more formal, others more dynamic.

I wondered how other pastors approach their daily and weekly demands, so I called a few to find out. Through a series of phone interviews, I discovered that pastors view their work through one of three paradigms: a weekly flow, a daily flow, or an 'ebb and flow.'

**Weekly Flow**

A popular model I encountered was touted by pastors who see their responsibilities in repeatable weekly rhythms. Earl Palmer, pastor of University Presbyterian Church, sees all of life this way. He believes that a weekly rhythm is the essence of a balanced life for all Christians, not just pastors.

"Until you can make sense out of seven days," Palmer says, "you can't make the most out of an individual day. That's the significance of the fourth commandment."

The beat of these rhythms is sounded by the days of each week. The divider tabs of a Daytimer are not only symbolic of this compartmentalized approach, they are a constant companion of those practicing it.

"I wouldn't dream of going anywhere without my personal

calendar," confided Don McCullough, pastor of Solana Beach Presbyterian Church. "Everything relating to my ministry and personal life is bound by those three silver rings."

His dividers separate daily appointments, prayer lists, sermon outlines, illustrations, expense reports, staff notes, and a phone directory. The days of his week are similarly categorized.

"Mondays are my days to deal with adminis-trivia. It's the only week day I handle correspondence. Tuesdays are devoted to basic sermon research and staff matters. Wednesday is my weekly window for creative expression; it's the day I work on a book manuscript, an article to be published, or lecture notes. Thursdays are protected for in-depth sermonizing, and Friday mornings are routinely carved out for writing the final sermon manuscript."

Palmer is also ruthless with his schedule: "I work incredibly hard and long Sunday through Wednesday so I have Thursday and Friday to devote entirely to my messages for this Sunday and the next. If you know what you're preaching next Sunday, you'll do a better job this week."

As one might expect reviewing these two schedules, both pastor large churches where much of the administration, counseling, and pastoral care is distributed among staff associates. Both men are primarily responsible for preaching and managing their staff.

But this approach need not be limited to large-church pastors. Rather than the size of the congregations or the number of paid staff, the key factor seems to be the pastor's desire to control his or her time. Leslie Krober, pastor of the Free Methodist Church in Wenatchee, Washington, began applying the weekly flow model long before his church attendance reached a thousand.

"I began reading material by Carl George of The Fuller Institute that challenged my tendencies to meet people's expectations, no matter how unrealistic," Krober recalls. "Because I don't like people to be upset with me or for programs to fall flat, I'd generally pick up the pieces others had dropped."

Carl George's metachurch philosophy struck a chord with Krober. It called for a style in which pastors manage ministry instead of reacting to it or doing it themselves. "I not only started carving out certain days of each week for certain tasks, but I also implemented my Big Blue system," said Krober.

Big Blue is a large, blue folder Krober keeps on the corner of his desk for calls, letters, projects, or requests that find their way to his office during the week. Rather than yielding to the temptation to drop everything and respond immediately, Krober throws the items into Big Blue and browses through them on the morning assigned to administration.

"When I finally respond to an 'urgent' matter," said Krober, "often the problem has already resolved itself. In the meantime, my Big Blue system has given me protracted sermon time during the week."

Gordon Kirk, pastor of Lake Avenue Congregational Church in Pasadena, California, agrees: if a congregation buys into the idea that ministry is not the exclusive domain of the pastor, believes Kirk, any pastor can make the weekly flow system work.

"When surrounded by a team of colleagues," Kirk insists, "opportunity for rhythmic blocks exist in every pastor's week. That team can be paid staff or volunteer staff. If ministry demands are shared, sufficient blocks of time can be assigned to preparing for Sunday morning."

Those who follow a weekly flow can't imagine life any other way. If there is any drawback to the method, though, it might be the curse of the large church. For Don McCullough, managing a multiple staff and a 2,000-attender church sometimes feels like being an executive of a major corporation rather than a pastor: "I catch myself wondering if I'm available enough for individuals within the congregation or if I'm too protected by my priorities."

### Daily Flow

The second popular paradigm is the more traditional daily cycle. In a given week, each day, except for the day off, resembles another. Mary Miller, associate pastor of First Wayne Street United Methodist Church in Fort Wayne, Indiana, embraces this pattern.

"After I drop my daughter off at daycare, my work day begins around 8:30 A.M. with devotions in my study," Miller says.

"Attempting a quiet time at home with a 2 year old hugging my knees is unrealistic."

From there, her typical day unwinds. She clears off her desk and addresses issues that have surfaced overnight. Then she closes her door to capture an hour or two of uninterrupted study time. By afternoon she is ready to handle correspondence, return calls, and do visitation.

Miller adds, "As long as I can find study blocks each day, my message is done by Thursday evening, so I can enjoy my Friday day off."

Also employing the daily flow method, Carl Taylor, pastor at Buffalo Covenant Church near Minneapolis, finds he studies best away from the phone and drop-in church visitors. "Before I go to the church, I have personal devotions and do reading for my sermon," says Taylor.

By ten o'clock he is ready to tackle administrative and staff-related responsibilities at the church campus. "Each staff member has a bit of my time every day," he says. "In a church of 500 members, the staff does much of the work. I spend much of my time pastoring them."

Although his afternoons vary, depending on who requests an appointment or which shut-in requires a visit, each day is remarkably the same. Administration, pastoral care, counseling, and discipleship occupy a bit of his calendar every day. Evening commitments take Taylor away from home an average of five nights a week. He is either overseeing various committees, counseling an engaged couple, or facilitating a Bible study.

Russ Carlson, pastor of North Haven Church in Cuyahoga Falls, Ohio, likes the rhythm of handling bits and pieces of his pastoral kit everyday. Similarly to Taylor and Miller, he protects his morning hours for study time. In addition, he takes five days twice a year to outline six months worth of Sunday messages.

Carlson observes, "That intensive time of prayer and anticipation holds my year together. When the unexpected knocks me out of synch with my daily regimen, the clippings, thoughts, and ideas accumulated since the study week guarantee I'll have something to say on Sunday."

The daily flow advantages are at least two:

● *Sermon preparation is distributed over the entire week.* If every day has study time built into it, the task of constructing a sermon is distributed over an entire week as opposed to two days.

Taylor muses, "I preach best when I orient my devotions around the Sunday text and allow the overflow of a week of personal worship to spill over into the pulpit."

Miller confesses, "I used to let the sermon go to the end of the week — you know, inspiration motivated by deadlines! The problem was that by waiting until the weekend to birth a sermon, I wasn't allowing the message to become a part of me."

Mary aims to finish by Thursday, so the message can circulate inside her at home on Friday and Saturday. Most of her best illustrations or sub-points, she claims, ambush her on her home days, when she isn't consciously thinking about Sunday morning: "I've preached more than one sermon flagged with yellow Post-it notes."

● *It guarantees a time for appointments each day.* This allows people access to their pastor without having to wait until "appointment day" the following week. A common daily routine keeps people in full view so their needs punctuate all the week's pastoral tasks. "My style," confides Taylor, "is to make myself available whenever people need to see me."

But there is a disadvantage to the daily flow method: unexpected calls and drop-ins often mess up the schedule. Daily flow pastors can be so committed to accomplishing their plans for a given day that when the unanticipated interrupts the daily schema, their day often extends late into the night. Because their day boundaries aren't as rigid as the weekly flow folks, daily flow people can easily attempt too much in a given day.

Because most people are only free in the evenings, Carl Taylor admits to but one free night a week. He has found that if he isn't careful, consecutive nights at the church result in tensions in his marriage.

For health reasons, Russ Carlson has taken concrete measures to counter his tendency toward workaholism. Early in his seminary studies, he was introduced to the daily flow model with an interesting twist. Russ simply calls it the "twelve-unit thing."

Here's how it works. Every week consists of twenty-one potential work units of three or four hours each: seven days times three (mornings, afternoons, and evenings). The maximum goal for any one week is to work twelve of those units (or about forty-eight hours).

For Carlson a typical week finds him putting in three units each on Mondays and Wednesdays when he has commitments through the day and evening. He takes Tuesday off and works mornings and afternoons Thursday and Friday — two units each day — and then works two more units on Sunday. (A social evening with people from the church also counts as a work unit).

Not only does this breakdown allow him to have most Saturdays free, it also protects four nights a week for his wife and three small children.

"I'm especially pleased with this system," Carlson said. "It is a tangible way of measuring my work as well as my worth. By looking at the units checked off, I can feel good about putting in a good amount of work. I also can give myself permission to quit. I don't feel guilty. After all, there are twelve units blacked out on my chart."

His wife likes the system, too. When she wonders out loud if he is giving her and the kids their fair share, she can look at his chart (which he fills out first thing every Monday morning) and decide with him if "repentance" is required.

When an unanticipated emergency pirates him away from his plan, Carlson's unit count for that week may total thirteen or fourteen. But then he gives himself permission to compensate the following week by reducing his units to ten or eleven.

For Earl Palmer, that's another reason why thoughtful rhythms, whether weekly or daily, should be taken seriously. "As long as you have a predictable pattern built into your ministry, you can handle the occasional crisis day. Subconsciously you know you can return to the rhythm represented by tomorrow."

The twelve-unit method may also be a means to combine the weekly flow and the daily flow model. Repeatable tasks can be assigned to each unit or series of units in a given week. For example, sermon preparation can be done in three units, every Tuesday afternoon and Wednesday and Thursday mornings.

## Ebb and Flow

Another schedule shrine to which many pastors bend the knee is what I call the ebb-and-flow model. I feel the freedom to name this category because I belong to it.

Whereas the weekly flow tends to characterize pastors leading large churches, ebb-and-flow pastors typically are found in churches of less than 400. However, the style has less to do with church size and more to do with priorities. As with the other models, this one is also distinguished by a pattern that defines each day. The pattern in this case is flexibility.

"Even though 75 percent of an average week consists of repeatable tasks, average weeks in my church are mostly rare." That church is Bethel Baptist Church in Concord, California, where Larry Baker pastors.

"Every day has its unique demands and wrinkles," he insists. An ebb-and-flow pastor like Baker has a loosely sketched weekly and daily plan. The bulletin tends to be written a certain day. The sermon is tackled at predictable hash marks of the week. The letters to visitors generally go out the first part of the week. But the distinguishing factor of the ebb-and-flow model is that people's needs take precedent over planned routines.

Unlike Don McCullough who only responds to correspondence on Mondays or Carl Taylor who has set times each day to return phone calls, ebb-and-flow pastors respond without delay (even when it means dropping their sermon preparation late in the week).

"Some of my best sermon illustrations," says Baker, "have come out of the emergencies that hijacked my preaching preparation. Responding at the moment connects me to the people for whom my sermon is intended."

I can relate. I resist being shackled by strait-jacket schedules. What will probably prevent me from pastoring a megachurch serves me well in a mid-sized church. People in pain know they have an advocate at the ready. An ebb-and-flow system is user friendly. The parishioner's whims win when I'm asked, "Is now a convenient time, Pastor?"

This model's advantage is its spontaneity. Ebb-and-flow people match their mood and energy level with any one of several tasks they must do before the week ends. In other words, every week is different even though the same things must be accomplished.

I attempt to write the bulletin and construct the order of worship on Tuesday afternoon (it's due on my secretary's desk Wednesday morning). But if my head is swimming from issues discussed at the staff meeting earlier in the day, I may not be ready to think through even my route home in rush-hour traffic, let alone plan Sunday's service. Often my heart is in a better place to orchestrate an order of worship after leading Tuesday night Bible study or before breakfast on Wednesday morning.

Baker speaks for this style's adherents when he says, "There is so much variety in my life, establishing a routine is difficult. What happens today bears little resemblance to what happened yesterday or what will undoubtedly occur tomorrow. The needs of a given day plus the deadlines of each week determine the only rhythm I require."

As you might have guessed, sophisticated calendar systems are not next-of-kin to ebb-and-flow pastors.

Tim McIntosh, pastor at Granville Chapel in Vancouver, British Columbia, carries his Seven-Star Diary with him most of the time. But he admits, "My datebook is more a place to jot notes than it is a prioritizer or planner. I keep most of my appointments in my head."

Although pastors worshiping the goddess of flexibility tend to like their approach, it's not without its drawbacks. Sure it's user friendly, but it also can be abuser friendly, too. I can't count the number of days each month I arrive at the church hoping for an uninterrupted morning of sermon preparation only to become the prisoner of those dreaded pink telephone messages. Before I realize what has happened, both the day and my energy have escaped, and Sunday's guillotine is one day closer.

McIntosh agrees, "Even though I am a spontaneous person and operate best without much structure, there are times when I desire to be more in control. Too often I feel I am controlled by paper and people."

According to my research, ebb-and-flow followers are least satisfied with their organization (or lack of it). There is an underlying desire to find a more lasting freedom than, ironically, flexibility affords them.

### Fitting in Personal Time

No matter the variety of routines, the high-wire act of ministry calls for balance. In all three paradigms, pastors contend with the demands between church and private life. None of the three systems guarantees balance.

All the pastors with whom I spoke valued their time with spouse and children. However, those following a weekly flow game plan, I observed, tended to be at home more evenings than those subscribing to the other two models. Typically, they are also early risers, at the church by 7 A.M., so when they come home for dinner, they have no need to return to church.

Family commitments realistic enough not to be consistently broken can act as balancing poles for those on the high wire.

Both Leslie Krober and Gordon Kirk make sure they have breakfast with their families (even if it means driving home from church and then returning). Don McCullough is always home for dinner with his wife and daughters: "That remains a constant even though my girls, who are now older, are off to their own evening commitments after we eat."

Weekly family traditions serve as a safety net beneath the high-tension wire of pastoral responsibilities.

Krober and his sons watch football together every Monday

night. Carl Taylor keeps special weekly dinner dates with his wife each Thursday and Friday. Palmer and his wife generally get away to their beach house on Thursdays for two nights (where he does his preparation for Sunday).

McCullough "lives" for pizza with the family on Saturday night. Says McCullough, "My weekend routine (which includes hitting the sack by 8 p.m. on Saturday so to be out of bed at 4 a.m. each Sunday) and our sense of balance is dependent on that traditional family circle of pepperoni and mushrooms. I actually believe pizza is one of the major food groups!"

Although most of those with whom I spoke tried taking Monday as their day off sometime in their careers, most do not anymore.

Larry Baker voices a common view: "After Sunday's intense responsibilities, I'm so drained and empty, I'm basically brain-dead on Mondays. I finally realized I was getting shorted by using the day after Sunday as the one day for me. So I switched: Mondays I now go into the office, meet with our seminary interns, and tackle tasks not requiring much concentration. By Friday, I've got a jump on Sunday morning, and my head is clear. It's a much better day than Monday to give my wife and children."

By the time McCullough has preached three times on Sunday morning, he experiences a similar emotional drop: "Dr. Archibald Hart at Fuller Seminary helped me understand that feeling incredibly low when our adrenal system has fueled us through a several-hour high is only normal. This old maxim applies: for every action there is an opposite and equal reaction. I have found that my recovery time is faster when I don't fight the depression and exhaustion that hits every Sunday afternoon. If I go home and collapse, not attempting to do anything else the rest of the day, by Monday I'm in better shape, able to get a good head start on my week."

Those with whom I spoke agreed that their effectiveness, efficiency, and enjoyment is leveraged by a day of leisure when they replenish their expended energy pool. For some it is a round of golf. For others it is lunch with their mate. For one it is a solitary sail in his boat on the bay. For another it is a novel or extended time over the newspaper. The day one chooses is not nearly as important as the discipline to take one.

And what of the pastor's need for solitude?

Richard Foster trumpets the need for recovery from racing routines in his classic, *Freedom of Simplicity*: "I function best when I alternate between periods of intense activity and of comparative solitude. When I understand this about myself, I can order my life accordingly. After a certain amount of immersion in public life, I begin to burn out. And I have noticed that I burn out inwardly long before I do outwardly. Hence I must be careful not to become a frantic bundle of hollow energy, busy among people but devoid of life. I must learn when to retreat like Jesus and experience the recreating power of God."

When I asked those I interviewed about their patterns for recreating, I heard throat clearing and the sound of brain cells turning somersaults.

Leslie Krober confessed, "I'm afraid I'm terrible at factoring in time for myself. I'm a compulsive people helper and problem solver. That's where my energy gravitates, even on my day off."

His is not the only energy that responds to that unilateral gravitational pull.

More than one pastor would relate to the simple joy that accompanies an attentive heart, which, in isolation, observes God's world. The poem, *Time For Me*, written anonymously, says it well:

Looking through my window
nature lies secure, untroubled, unpressured, calm.
Deeply rooted trees standing upright
rustle in the breeze graceful, quietly being.

Today I feel one with them
no pressure, no people, no distractions, just time.
Time to sit, to think,
to let thoughts drift by
pausing on one here or there sifting, sorting, weighing.

In the quietness I see clearly,
make decisions, reach conclusions.

I feel more complete, sense of satisfaction in
   having time for me.

Apparently most of us are still struggling to make space for
such uncluttered time.

## Time Is Sacred

Although differences existed in the way they viewed their
weeks, most pastors I spoke with shared one significant belief: time
is sacred and worthy of respect.

Unless the hours in a week are harnessed meaningfully, they
become a wasted natural resource. Time waits for no one; time returns
for no one. Pastors weep along with everyone else when, before we
show up, the majesty of the moment has been dethroned. We grieve
lost opportunities with our congregations, and we regret lost moments with our families.

In his book, *In Praise of Play: Toward a Psychology of Religion*,
R. E. Neale noted, "Nothing is more characteristic of modern man
than the complaint, 'If only I had time.' "

Christian apologist Michael Quoist adds, "Life is more hectic
than we prefer it to be. We pause to regret this every so often but
then rush off to attend to whatever is next on our list of responsibilities. But we treat it as a fact of life rather than as a condition that can
be changed. And we seldom regard the condition as one which we
have had a significant part in shaping."

Recently during a worship service, I interviewed a mail carrier
in our community whose life story was written up in the newspaper. His love for his job is easily observed by those who are on the
receiving end of his route. Flip Feeney is not just a mailman; he's a
"pastor" with a letter pouch.

During the interview, Flip suggested a way for people to enjoy
their work more. They should dissect a sheet of paper with a vertical
line and then list the things they like about their work in the left
column. They then should list the things they don't like on the right
side.

"Change what you don't like about what you do or change the

way you do it," Flip concluded. "If you can't make any changes, find another job."

I am beginning to evaluate just how satisfied I am with my ebb-and-flow identity. I know I have the ability to change if I really want to. The question remains: "What plan will make me more effective and a better steward of my time?"

Carl Taylor suggests we begin answering that question by identifying our areas of personal strength and giftedness and then experimenting with ways those muscles can be flexed.

Don McCullough, though, cautions against simply accommodating our strengths. For McCullough, the more realistic word is "balance."

"In every church situation we are called to do certain things that may or may not be something we do particularly well," he says. "It is just part of our call. To the degree that need matches giftedness, that's great! Realistically though, we need to discover what it is we can uniquely contribute to this congregation in light of what they need. Once we've done that, we can organize our time as best we can so to invest our unique abilities and focus on those tasks that depend on us."

Discovering our rhythm is much like jogging. When I'm in my stride, I'm oblivious to the pavement, the perspiration, and the pain. I feel I could challenge any world-class marathoner. But I don't always find my stride before the run is done. When I do, it's because I am conscious of various aspects of my body working.

There is no guarantee we will find the stride in our schedules unless we pay close attention to the issue of balance. However, in listening to those who have found their stride, there is no joy that compares with finding a rhythm that works for you.

*PART THREE*
# Time with Others

---

*To be effective outside the church, in the community, people inside the church must get along.*
— Greg Asimakoupoulos

# CHAPTER EIGHT

# Working Efficiently with People

The infection set in shortly after he arrived at the church. A highly gifted associate, Todd started his Christian education ministry the same weekend our second daughter was born. Both events were celebrated as answers to prayer and appeared equally promising.

Nine months had changed everything, however. Whereas I eagerly anticipated each evening greeting my daughter, Allison, I got a knot in my stomach each morning anticipating bumping into Todd.

We didn't see eye to eye on many things. My hands-on

leadership style frustrated him; his use of time drove me nuts. He questioned my annoyance with his laid-back attitude and struggled to follow through on projects; I struggled to communicate openly with him. Though the congregation was oblivious to our five-year allergic reaction, by the time the rash was visible, the dis-ease required radical surgery. He eventually left the church.

To be effective outside the church, to the community, people inside the church must get along. Attending to those doing the work of the ministry, as I painfully learned, can be done inefficiently, grinding the wheels of ministry to a noisy halt.

I've since discovered it doesn't have to be that way.

### From Infirmary to Injury

Sentenced to a starkly furnished hospital waiting room, I confined my solitary thoughts to the events down the closed-off corridor. My 63-year-old father was in surgery to repair the damage of a near fatal heart attack. Five hours and four by-passes later, the surgeon spoke the words for which we had hoped: Dad would pull through.

But relief quickly dissolved to fear: a staph infection contracted in the hospital threatened his recovery. I had thought modern medical centers were citadels of sterility. What I did not know, however, is that almost as many people die each year from infections contracted in hospitals as from the illnesses for which they are hospitalized.

Instead of healing, this hospital contaminated my father, undermining the institution's purpose. Fortunately, my dad recovered from his lingering infection. But too often, churches, like hospitals, endanger the health of its constituents. Health is also a church issue. Dis-ease among staff and volunteers can be a fatal distraction.

After Todd's resignation, two years passed before our congregation restabilized. In retrospect, early detection and treatment would have been possible had I implemented the following:

● *A complete physical.* Unfortunately, I possessed little experience in staff relationships. I had served as an associate once, but this was my first time recruiting a staff member. I had stumbled through

Todd's candidating process. I was unaware of the myriad personality inventories that analyze work habits and forecast potential areas of conflict.

If only we had both been x-rayed early on, the shadows on our good intentions would have been detected. We could have agreed to cut off discussions at the candidating phase or determined that occupational therapy would be sought from the beginning.

● *A daily regimen.* An associate's job description should be detailed beyond what seems necessary. Uncommunicated expectations generally translate into unacceptable performance. The last time I read 1 Corinthians 12, mind reading wasn't on the list of available spiritual gifts.

Neither is mime reading. Todd's job description did not specify office hours, so I attempted to model appropriate work habits. At times I felt like Charlie Chaplin penguining around the office, hoping to motivate Todd by my long hours and visibility. But he didn't pick up on my cues. Exhausted and resentful, I picked up a bad attitude.

When I hired my next staff member, I assumed nothing. I made sure the minute details of his job description included office procedures, weekly time minimums, weekend and evening expectations, and an accountability structure. Although I felt self-conscious about what seemed like detailed and high expectations, I swallowed hard and discussed it openly with the candidate. To my amazement he appreciated the thoroughness of the listed expectations.

Scott was an experienced youth pastor. He was familiar with a myriad of team ministry models, but he had his preferences. His performance was enhanced by a job description he knew fit him.

"A snug uniform fits me best," he said while looking over the prospectus of the position. "Too loose a fit is uncomfortable — leaves too much room for doubt. I like a coach who has a game plan for each player. As long as I know what is expected of me, let me on the field, and look out!"

Later, when trust is earned, the demands of a job description can be relaxed. But knowing what is expected does relieve staff members from the anxiety of wondering if they are doing too little or too much.

• *Frequent office visits.* I dropped the ball with Todd. What I should have dropped was my pen. Instead of expressing my concerns or complaints in person, I wrote memos and slid them under his door. My own insecurities couldn't handle rejection, so I avoided the messy matter. Had I regularly dropped by Todd's office for friendly chats and ministry updates, our relationship would have endured face-to-face discussions about unmet expectations.

I now work with five other staff members. We insist upon weekly checkups. Staff meetings are a must. To maintain a common heartbeat, there is an obvious need for structured evaluation, planning, and prayer. Maintaining quality staff times is not easy, but valuable efforts rarely are.

I've discovered that water-cooler conversations and chit-chat in an associate's office are just as profitable as two-hour staff meetings. Talking on their turf underscores our equally important roles in ministry. Informal give-and-take builds trust. As far as they're concerned, I can't chew the fat too often. And gratefully, I've learned it sure beats chewing someone out.

I was first introduced to this corrective technique by a retired conference superintendent named Clarence. What made him effective as a denominational executive I found described in Peters and Waterman's management classic, *In Search of Excellence.* Successful managers are not chained to their desks. They budget time for banter. "Management by walking around" Peters and Waterman call it. Clarence called it "ministry the Master's way."

Wandering around the office is an aerobic exercise that prevents bad blood from circulating among the staff.

• *House calls.* Marcus Welby isn't the only one who makes routine home visits. So does a senior pastor worth his smelling salt. Staff families need to be in each other's homes if rapport and trust are to be nurtured.

If this marriage axiom is true — you marry your spouse's family, not just your spouse — the same is true in staff relationships. Staff families can support the excitement of the ministry only to the degree they can relate to one another.

Here was another area of my negligence with Todd. Whereas we saw each other every day, our wives and children had only a superficial relationship. Sunday contact was not sufficient to bond our families, to own the common vision. When deadlines demanded overtime and additional sacrifice, the reservoir of trust, understanding, and support was empty.

### Getting It Off Your Chest

Infection spreads when it goes untreated. Todd and I also neglected to treat our frustrations. Our need to smile and lead Sunday morning worship side-by-side conspired against an honest admission of paralyzing conflict.

To use a Chuck Swindoll analogy, we behaved like porcupines. When we got in a tight situation, our quills pricked each other. We'd back off to avoid the pain each other's presence caused, going our separate ways. But the chill of ministry drew us to seek companionship's warmth. Drawing near with unresolved hostilities, however, we soon were rubbing each other raw.

My reluctance to communicate what I really thought — my frustrations, resentments, emotional burnout — contributed to my nine-month bout with clinical depression. I became the victim of an emotional stroke. My faith drooped, and my feelings disappeared. Unexpressed anger and resentment could not be allowed to build without burping bile after a while.

I am learning how to communicate my frustrations. I have my secretary to thank. She doesn't bottle her feelings or carry a bottle of Tums. It's never a secret when she is troubled by something I've said or done. She takes the initiative and asks, "There's something on my mind. Can we talk about it?" Her example is enabling me to talk instead of balk.

Several questions now help me monitor my feelings toward those with whom I work: Are there knots in my stomach when I arrive at work? If so, what do they signal? Does my tardiness point to a deeper issue: a passive resistance toward someone in the office? Does my "radar" detect an emotional distancing between another staff member and me? Is it possible he or she has misunderstood something I said or did?

### Assuming the Best

I was much better at making notations in the debit column of Todd's chart than on the credit side. And while I'm no psychologist, I think I know why.

For many of my childhood years, my dad managed residential properties. I observed him age prematurely as he dealt with irresponsible tenants and trashed apartments. As I entered adulthood, I think I subconsciously viewed people critically. Rather than giving them the benefit of the doubt, I questioned their integrity. No one could be trusted.

To make matters worse, while in college, I worked for a man who reinforced my assumptions. A negative, lugubrious employer, he never acknowledged good effort. But when I blew it, he made sure I knew about his displeasure.

Perhaps both environments tainted me. As a result, Todd was more apt to hear about my reaction to a project when I wasn't pleased than when I was. What I have since come to understand is not only my bias but a proven managerial maxim: Most people want to do their best. They are motivated by opportunities for success and affirmation.

In their book, *Manage Your Time, Manage Your Work, Manage Yourself,* Douglass and Donna Merrill say, "People tend to live up to what is expected of them. If poor performance is expected, poor performance will be delivered. If great accomplishments are called for, these too will be delivered. Learn to have faith in and respect for your employees; you will be the winner and so will they."

When our church hired a husband-wife Christian education team, I tried the Merrills' approach. Because the husband-wife team had just completed graduate work in education, I knew they were more in step with such issues than I was. While I communicated certain expectations, I assumed the best, standing back and letting them prove themselves.

When I mentally questioned their timing or approach, I bit my tongue and bided my time. I cheered their efforts and checked my former ways. My supervisory role, I discovered, was to identify and remove any blocks impeding their ability to do their best.

I am also recognizing my role as cheerleader. It was Mark Twain who said, "There is only 18 inches between a slap on the back and a slap on the posterior, but oh what a difference those 18 inches make!"

Positive performance deserves praise, and praise perpetuates performance. I now keep my pom-poms in my front desk drawer.

### Nine Habits for Highly Effective Volunteers

But what about those who don't punch a time clock?

In many respects, managing volunteers and paid staff members requires similar skills, so there is some overlap. For instance, both are motivated by praise. Still, I've made several other discoveries that help me keep volunteers motivated and our relationship healthy.

*1. Appreciation.* Even more than paid staff, volunteers need recognition. When we supplemented our church office with eight receptionists, who each donate four hours once a week, we provided each with a name plate. Each week when they come to work, they slide their names into the holder on the reception desk.

We also make them feel important by giving them a sense of ownership in the church's mission. Public praise from the pulpit, hand-engraved certificates, newsletter recognition, customized thank-you cards are a few of the ways volunteers in our church are compensated.

I've found it especially tempting to focus on their work only, to the exclusion of the volunteers themselves. Though delaying a project awaiting me, the few minutes I inquire about a volunteer's weekend or family or a recent prayer request makes a difference, giving the volunteer an emotional boost.

*2. Flexibility.* For years we struggled to find people who would commit to teach Sunday school twelve months straight. Finally, when we opted for a rotating schedule (each teacher gets every other month off), we had more than enough volunteers from which to draw.

Our system may not resemble textbook recruitment, but it is more sensitive to the hectic lifestyles of our members. As you can see, we use a similar philosophy in recruiting receptionists.

3. *Extra guidelines.* Uncertainty breeds anxiety and dissipated energy. Volunteers must be able to restate what they think you want them to do. Thoughts unattached to paper are too slippery for comfort. Job descriptions drawn up on paper aren't just for those drawing a salary.

The ushers' job description is a good example. As part of the recruitment process in our church, ushers are given guidelines and expectations (in addition to a training session). Each usher is assigned to a rotating monthly schedule. Four Sundays on, four Sundays off. They are asked to wear a shirt, tie, and suit or sport coat, and arrive 15 minutes before the service. They are encouraged to carry breath mints. Their duties include distributing bulletins with a smile, assisting those who have difficulty finding a seat, and collecting the offering. Following worship they are requested to pick up loose papers and tidy the sanctuary.

4. *Authority and responsibility.* Contented workers are those who know a project is theirs to complete. They know the pastor will not step in and take control once the assignment has been given.

When one missions conference was still four months off, I sat with the missions chairman. After agreeing on the theme and desired outcomes of the month-long event, I felt comfortable leaving the details to Martin and his committee. Their enthusiasm and conscientiousness in past conferences earned my trust.

When it was all over, the committee beamed with a sense of accomplishment. Their pride was well-deserved. The speakers they had chosen were top notch. The way they had creatively expressed the theme was remarkable. The narthex resembled an international airport terminal complete with a metal detector through which people passed to enter the sanctuary. My willingness to keep hands off resulted in a contagion that carried the committee to do it again the next year.

5. *Extra time.* Time management is not just the struggle of paid professionals. Volunteers are juggling full-time jobs and family and ministry responsibilities. These issues occupy volunteers' minds and consume energy. That can interfere with the church task you expect them to complete.

In our church, some office helpers need as much as half an hour to settle in and get their minds on the job. Some will brew coffee, make small talk, and flip through the church newsletter before they're ready to type a letter or file minutes.

I not only need to be patient and flexible, I also try to be more generous with deadlines. That may shortcircuit efficiency, but workers enjoy their work more, and I've found that more gets done in the long run. That's the kind of realistic clock that ticks with those who don't punch one.

6. *A professional feel.* Recently I asked the head of our volunteer receptionists for her insights on how I might respond better to a troubled church member she knows well. Not only did she give me good advice, she left her work station feeling she had contributed to the overall ministry of the church.

So I've found that if volunteer staff are not included in regular pastoral staff meetings, at least they should be consulted. They need to feel their opinions and performance are respected and expected.

7. *Free to fail.* Our church chairman was a military officer for over twenty-five years. He serves on the church council, leads a home Bible study, and teaches Sunday school. In all of his commitments, he has tried a lot of novel programs. Not all of them have succeeded.

Nonetheless, he has a reputation in our church for being a successful leader. He has taught me that volunteers can be motivated by wrong choices. He gives himself permission to make mistakes. He's been influenced by retired Rear Admiral Grace Hopper of the Navy, who claimed, "It is always easier to get forgiveness than to get permission." Steve's outlook is much the same. He has a readiness to risk.

Two of his favorite sayings betray his approach to life. One he terms the eleventh commandment: "Thou shalt not sweat it." The other he places with the Beatitudes: "Blessed are those who have permission to change their minds."

Once Steve devised a great system for assimilating newer people into the life of the church. He contacted two or three established couples who agreed to host regular dinner parties to which the new people would be invited. Each month several new folks would be enfolded. It sounded like a terrific idea.

However, it failed to weather the brainstorm. The hosts couldn't find free nights in common with the newcomers. The visitors were not as willing to be assimilated as we had assumed. Rather than trying to make a foiled idea fly, Steve quickly admitted defeat and went on to some other approach. Because he was undaunted, I was too. Because he gave himself permission to fail, I've learned to give the same to others.

As long as you are working with people who know what success tastes like, you can give them the freedom to fall short. If you aren't sure what a volunteer is capable of, delegate a task to her you can afford for her to mess up.

8. *Regular time off.* Whether they're payroll- or cinnamon-roll-rewarded workers, it doesn't matter. Church work is people work, and people work leaves people pooped.

Sunday school teachers, encouraged to take the summer off from teaching are more inclined to re-up in the fall, refreshed, their emotional elastic back in shape. The same goes for volunteer custodial help, gardeners, greeters, or worship leaders. A breather is the best investment to guarantee a high-yield return.

9. *Regular celebrations.* At Crossroads, we look for reasons to have a party and seize the moment to recognize accomplishment.

It's not a novel idea. They do it in the hair salon where I get my hair cut. Every season of the year is recognized by contests, displays, and wall hangings. Sometimes they even wear costumes to celebrate a special day or occasion. The team of hair cutters obviously enjoys working together.

Those who find reasons to blow trumpets or blow up balloons will laugh more, complain less, and trust each other to a greater degree. All it takes is keeping my ears to the ground for noteworthy achievements and seizing the day.

### White-Knuckled Leadership

Several years ago while making a routine flight from Portland, Maine, to Boston, Henry Dempsey heard an unusual noise near the rear of his commuter aircraft.

Turning the controls over to his copilot, he walked to the back of the plane. As he reached the tail section, the plane hit an air pocket, and he was thrust against the rear door. Henry inadvertently discovered the source of the mysterious noise: the rear door had not been adequately latched. As the weight of Henry's body fell against the door, it flew open, and the unsuspecting pilot was sucked out of the jet.

The copilot, detecting the open door on the instrument panel, radioed the nearest control tower, requesting permission to land, reporting that his colleague had fallen out of the plane.

Henry, however, had managed to grab the outdoor ladder at the rear of the plane. He clung to a rung with his bare hands while the plane maintained a speed of 200 miles per hour and descended from 4,000 feet.

Ten minutes later the jet landed. Henry's head was a mere twelve inches off the tarmac. According to the newspaper report I read, prying his fingers from the ladder took airport personnel several minutes.

Holding on for Henry was a matter of life or death. Likewise, when the bumpiness of ministry threatens to toss me into an oblivion of wrecked schedules and misplaced priorities, I am wise to retain a grip, especially on the few key tasks that center around people ministry. If I let go of them, I've found I may not only have to let go of staff members, I essentially let go of productive ministry. When I failed to spend adequate time creating a spirit of unity with my associate Todd, the synergism of growth declined.

Benign neglect erodes the magnetic draw of our influence, and then we remain leaders in name only. As Christian management consultant Fred Smith has chided, "He who thinks he is leading and turns around to find nobody following him is simply out for a walk."

Helping people work efficiently is no summer vacation. It is a year-long job, unpredictable as an August day in Seattle. The only predictable element is that it's time intensive. As long as people are involved, people will be people, and prayers for patience will never be answered soon enough. As some pastor said, "The ministry would be a piece of cake if it wasn't for people!"

Maybe so. But working with people and their unpredictable pain is ministry. And that's why I'll never pastor a perfect church, lead a perfect staff, or work a forty-hour week.

*What happens in a meeting is decided before the meeting, by the process.*

— *John Maxwell*

# CHAPTER NINE

# Making the Most of Meetings

---

Two weeks before beginning a pastorate in Lancaster, Ohio, I attended my new church's business meeting. The outgoing pastor had informed me the church would be voting on a hot issue: whether to build an activity building. So I drove to Lancaster, slipped into the church after the meeting had begun, and went upstairs to the balcony to watch.

What I saw depressed me. Christians fought and yelled like children. The ruckus began when a man named Bill, a well-known saboteur of church business meetings, stood and used a familiar ploy. He raised a procedural question that the pastor didn't know how to handle. Bill then rattled off chapter and verse from *Robert's Rules of Order* and before sitting down intoned, "I hope the rest of this meeting can be run more competently."

That parliamentary move set the tone for a four-hour meeting that felt more like a beating.

Meetings bring out the best — and worst — in us. Egos, hidden agendas, poor planning, aimlessness, temper tantrums, and boredom can come obnoxiously into play. On the other hand, meetings can be a showcase of Christian grace, courtesy, vision, planning, enthusiasm, and hope.

Depending on which carries the day, a pastor's ministry purrs along or screeches to a halt in board meetings, business meetings, staff meetings, committee meetings, training meetings. They either multiply your time, like a compact car getting 50 miles to the gallon, or devour time and energy, like a gas-guzzling, exhaust-belching, old bus.

Here's how to "adjust the carburetor" of your church to get more done, in less time, in a positive manner.

### A Conspicuous Absence

What pastor hasn't sat in a committee meeting thinking, *How can I get out of attending this every month? If I quit coming, they'll think I don't care or that I'm negligent. But I'm wasting my time!*

When I came to Skyline Church in San Diego, the church had fifteen committees, and I was expected to attend every one. I quickly discovered I didn't need to be at any of them. Here are principles I followed to reduce to zero the number of committees I attend.

• *Report your new policy in person.* I attended every committee meeting in the church — once — and told them I would not be back. Obviously when you stop attending a meeting, committee members may feel unimportant. That feeling would have been heightened if I had just sent a memo or phoned the leader about my change in policy. I wanted to show the participants I respected them enough to talk face to face.

• *Explain your reasons.* Once people see the big picture of a pastor's schedule, they understand better. To each committee I said something like this: "I won't be attending this committee for two reasons. First and most important, I have complete confidence in your ability to get the job done, and so I'm turning you loose. Second, my time is limited. If I attend fifteen committees every month, my preaching, administration, leadership, and family life will suffer. It's a matter of priorities."

● *Delegate decisions and problem-solving to the lowest level possible.* Many churches do the opposite, with the church board deciding everything from what light bulbs to buy to who should screw them in. Giving committees real authority makes their work important. Most members appreciate not having to work in my shadow.

Each committee chairman is on the board, so as I develop a close relationship with my board through discipleship sessions and personal lunches, I also develop a close tie with their committee efforts. The committee chairpersons are always aware of their place in the scheme of things and of their importance to me.

● *Anticipate diverse reactions.* When I made the rounds of our fifteen committees, I found that the activist committees, those anxious to get something done, felt great about my not attending. They were free to get on with their thing. More relational groups were upset; they saw meetings as a time to be with their pastor.

● *Don't overrule committee decisions.* Our Christian education committee has the authority to recommend personnel in their department. When we needed to fill a position several years ago, they submitted the name of one of our volunteer workers. The person recommended was a hard worker but not, in my and the board's judgment, leadership material. The board was unanimous in opposition to the name submitted.

During my eleven years here, however, our board hasn't overruled a single decision of a committee. If committees have their decisions overruled by the board, members soon realize what they do doesn't matter.

So we asked the chairman of the Christian education committee, who is on the board, to go back, explain our thinking, and ask the committee to consider overruling their decision. When he did, the members of his group recognized the wisdom of the board and withdrew the name voluntarily.

On rare occasions when the board resists a committee decision, we keep the authority in the hands of the committee, asking them to reconsider, rather than just rejecting it. By not overruling their decisions, I communicate they are important.

● *Show the committee you're up on their work.* We've whittled the number of committees from fifteen to four, and have the four committee chairpersons on the board. So I have a lot of contact with these leaders. But I also take the time to read the minutes of each committee. I also jot notes to the chairpersons to tell them the good things I see happening in their committees.

### Meeting of the Minds

More than any other group on this planet, church members meet just to meet. That's natural considering our bond in Christ. That's wonderful for relationships, but it's murder on schedules and priorities. Churches are infamous for scheduled meetings that have no objectives, no announced purpose, with people invited for the wrong reasons. The result is a fleeting of the minds.

To counteract this tendency, our board meetings must have three clearly defined purposes.

*1. Information and empowerment.* I start board meetings with five to ten minutes of reports on good things happening in the church: "Last month fifteen people dedicated their lives to Christ. Two of those people were a husband and wife about to file for divorce, and they decided to stay together. . . ."

I empower people with vision, motivation, enthusiasm, and faith. We celebrate that, through Christ, our church is winning and that each person in attendance is part of the reason why.

I recently invited to my house our building steering committee of forty-eight people. When we sat down in the library, I said, "Four years from now we'll be in the new sanctuary. Four thousand people will be praising God in that building, but you forty-eight will be able to appreciate the Lord's goodness more than anyone else."

Then we called the leader of the relocation committee

forward, laid hands on him, and prayed for him. He called the office the next day and said, "I've never had an experience like that. It has changed my life. If you had any doubts about whether I'm completely involved in this project, I just want to say, 'Aye, aye, aye, yes, yes, yes!' "

Discipleship is another necessary part of empowerment, but we don't take time for it in our regular board meeting. I meet for discipleship once a month with my board, on Saturday morning from eight to ten. We eat breakfast for the first half-hour and then move to Scripture study, prayer, and discussing our personal lives. Last year our theme was intimacy with Christ, and this year we're studying Psalms.

*2. Brainstorming, information gathering, and discussion.* What I call "study items" take about an hour and fifteen minutes of our board meeting. We make no decisions on study items. Some issues will remain study items for months.

Regular board meetings don't provide enough time for everything that needs attention. At our board administration retreat, we take board members and their spouses for a day and focus on two to four big issues. I throw a question that needs brainstorming on the table and let everyone have at it. Last year the question was whether we should add a fourth service. We'll often break for thirty minutes into discussion groups of four, then come together and relate the ideas generated. This isn't a decision-making day; it's just a gleaning of ideas.

*3. Decision making.* This is my last priority at board meetings. We end with two to five minutes of what I call "action items." These have been study items in previous meetings that we're ready to vote on.

Voting is not a big deal at board meetings because I know before I go in what the vote will be — unanimous. I know ahead of time because of the "people process."

### The People Process

As they try to bring about change, church leaders tend to be event oriented: they focus on board and congregational meetings as the turning points of the church. They put all their eggs in the basket of one sermon or presentation to rally the congregation behind them. That outlook fosters frustration, crises, surprises, and power plays.

Viewing leadership as a process of moving people in a desired direction is more realistic and effective. Change takes time.

Three factors are critical to the people process.

• *Consensus.* After that four hours of horrendous congregational debate I mentioned in the introduction, the church in Lancaster voted by a two-thirds majority to build a new activity building. The third who lost the vote felt like losers, and a split resulted. They didn't leave the church physically, but they did emotionally and financially.

When I came, I knew we had to bring them back on board. I also wanted to delay the building project because the church was planning to build on a spot where I foresaw a new sanctuary (once the church was growing again). So I told the leaders, "This activities building is important. It's obvious there are strong feelings on both sides. I suggest we form a study committee and come back to the issue later."

They agreed. I appointed phlegmatic personalities to the committee and instructed them, "I want a detailed study. Take your time. Don't come back until you have the whole picture for us."

The church began to move and grow. Nine months later, when the committee reported their findings to the congregation, we reconsidered whether to build an activity building or a new sanctuary. Only one person voted against building a sanctuary.

That congregational meeting, however, wasn't the turning point. The church changed direction because of a process of talking to people one-to-one, changing little things here and there, building vision piece-by-piece, bringing one group on board at a time.

Actually, when it comes to decision making, meetings should hold no surprises. You can only do this if you have the right decision-making process. In our board meetings, the simple mechanism of dividing issues into study items and action items not only processes issues but people. By barring an immediate vote on study items, we take away the political pressures — people don't have to take sides immediately. In fact I'm careful to lead discussions in a way that keeps people from declaring their position on an issue.

Once a person takes a stand and raises her flag, she feels obligated to defend that position even if she eventually sees the wisdom of doing otherwise. Changing your mind is like saying you were wrong, and most people don't like to do that. So we discuss issues not in terms of "What do you think we should do?" but with questions like "What are the pros and cons of doing this?" and "What are the advantages and disadvantages of each of these solutions?"

Weighty issues can remain study items for months. Along the way I get a feeling where everyone stands. Only when I sense consensus do we move a study item to an action item for the next month's meeting.

Six years after the church in Lancaster built their new sanctuary, we addressed the issue of what to do with the old one. I wanted to make it an activities building (it had a rectangular shape and a high ceiling throughout, perfect for a gym), but I knew how tradition-conscious members of the congregation would react: "The foul line of the basketball court will be at the altar where I prayed to receive Christ."

So I began with a study item. "We're not going to vote on this tonight, next month, or the month after. But let's think about what we could do with the old sanctuary. Any idea will be fine. It can be far-fetched; it can be stupid. Let's just get them on the table." We wrote down all the ideas on a blackboard and then left it at that.

We left that as a study item for eight months. Every month we talked about it, and I watched as the process of communication changed minds one by one.

• *Leading leaders.* After the sanctuary-use question had been a study item for eight months, I took the vice-chairman of the board out for lunch, as I regularly did, to discuss the meeting. He had led the anti-gym wing, but I sensed he had softened. At lunch I asked directly what he felt.

"Well," he said, "I think it should be a gym."

"I think you're right," I responded. "But I've kept this as a study item because I wanted you to be with me on it. And the only way I'll move it to an action item is if you're ready to lead the way with a motion."

He agreed. The next month the board voted unanimously to convert the building to a gym, and in the congregational meeting people voted 98 percent in favor.

The key to leadership is influencing those who influence others. Influencers are in every congregation, and they determine much of what happens in meetings. You have to know who they are. They are the ones whose opinions matter most, whose views others listen to and respect. When they are ignored or overlooked, or when a pastor does an end-around, they lead the opposition and make a pastor's life miserable.

A grim church member presented a pastor with a six-page list of misdemeanors. The letter criticized him because his car was too expensive, he didn't visit one individual at home, he didn't preach enough from the Old Testament, he didn't support Sunday school by teaching a class himself, his wife set a bad example by missing church several Sunday nights a year. . . . A list of complaints like that is often nothing more than an influencer left out of the "power loop."

Likewise, you can trace many major church conflicts to a prominent influencer who doesn't like the pastor. The dissenter's beef isn't doctrinal. It's not cultural. Often he or she has felt left out of a critical decision.

Consequently, I prepare for meetings by preparing the players. I spend five hours preparing for every hour of a meeting, praying, getting the mind of the Lord, making decisions, planning the agenda, and preparing people.

For instance, when I went to one conference, John, the vice-chairman, who actually moderates the board meetings, traveled with me. During the trip we discussed every board member, their strengths and gifts, the keys to their lives, what fires their engines. We were exploring people's interests and motivations to better understand how they would respond in a meeting. In addition we talked about who influenced each board member.

Then I suggested, "Of our sixteen board members, you need to keep in good relationship with these four. You need to know that they're with you on any issue you think we ought to present for a vote. If they're with you, the others will go along."

The pejorative word for the people process is *politics*. If a leader's motives are selfish, if he or she is working the process for the sake of power, if ego is the moving force, then this is politics in the negative sense. It's manipulation.

If, on the other hand, a leader is motivated by love for Christ, love for the church, and love for the individuals in the process, then the people process simply recognizes how people make decisions. If a leader respects others' freedom to choose and the time it takes them to choose, and if the leader refrains from twisting arms, then we are fulfilling our call to persuade and influence others for the sake of the kingdom. If our motives are right, we only have as much influence as people grant us.

Developing trust among influencers, then, is critical. On our trip to Atlanta, I told John, "I will never disagree with you in a meeting. We'll disagree before or after the meeting behind closed doors. I'll never embarrass you. I'll always build you up. Also, I will always pave the way so that motions you bring forward will pass. My goal is to make you look good; your goal is to know my heart and be loyal to that."

Not only do we need to give influencers influence, we need to give them credit. I tell John, "Great meeting. You did a good job leading us through the whole process."

Influencers either are or they aren't. You can't make someone into an influencer. One characteristic of all leaders I've met is an instinctive awareness of their influence in a group. Leaders are sensitive to power, they know who the other leaders are in a group, and they adjust to that. It doesn't mean they necessarily "love to be first," but they know where they stand.

My recognizing who is sensitive to influence is the first way I pick a leader and the first way I prepare for any meeting. If you understand who the influencers are in any meeting, and if you can relate well with them, it doesn't matter whether it's your church, General Motors, or the United States of America, you can run that meeting and that organization effectively.

● *Understanding people.* Leaders don't have bad meetings because they're inept with meetings; they have bad meetings because they're inept with people.

Someone who doesn't understand people can read all the management literature and apply the techniques for leading meetings but still have problems. The greatest leaders are not necessarily technically efficient at running meetings, at following step one, step two, and step three; they usually are artists.

Good meetings are based on the art of influencing people. I assume people are biased negatively against change. Most people will resist a new idea. Therefore if I'm going to lead in a new direction, it will take time. I know how long each member of my board takes to process information and make decisions. Some people are ready to act in five minutes. Others take two months.

Never pluck fruit before it's ready. If I pressure people, they may do what I want, but they'll resent it. That resentment becomes a wall between us, causing them to hold back whenever I try to influence again. When I wait for the fruit to drop, however, trust builds. People sense I won't take advantage of them or violate their integrity or emotional make-up.

The better I know the participants in meetings, the better I can lead those meetings. I spend time individually with board members, annually taking them to lunch or dinner, getting a feel for their hearts, their family lives, their jobs. I also get to know them in our monthly discipleship meetings, at the board social events we hold several times a year, and at our annual all-day retreat. I take board members on trips with me whenever possible.

Certain situations have higher potential for us getting to know one another. When we pray together, I learn people's hearts for God and their chief concerns. When we go through crises together, I see how they respond to pressure, and they see how I treat them under pressure. We develop a one-for-all and all-for-one feeling. When we win together, mutual confidence and trust develops.

## Reducing Drag

Paul Henri Spaak was president of the first General Assembly of the United Nations. After presiding over the first General Assembly meeting, Spaak closed with these words:

"Our agenda is now exhausted. The secretary general is exhausted. All of you are exhausted. I find it comforting that, beginning with our very first day, we find ourselves in such complete unanimity."

I am a mortal enemy of that kind of unanimity. If there's one thing I want, it's to finish meetings more energized and motivated than when I walked in. The only way to do that is to be brief. As the saying goes, work expands to fill the time allotted to it. If everyone assumes a board meeting should last late into the night, that's exactly what happens.

There are many reasons that meetings drag on, but one big one is when a few individuals dominate. They may not dominate maliciously, but they are too verbal, or they're emotionally troubled and want attention, or long-winded, or egotistical. Sometimes, the only way to get control of meetings, is to beat them at their own game.

Sitting in the balcony, watching the Lancaster church business meeting ruined by one man, a man who had a history of thwarting meetings by his supposed adherence to *Robert's Rules of Order*, I determined I would not let the same thing happen to me.

One year later I prepared for my first congregational meeting by spending three days studying *Robert's Rules*; I virtually memorized it.

Sure enough, Bill stood in the meeting and tried to get a motion passed, saying that a simple majority would do. I knew, though, that his motion required a two-thirds majority.

"You can't do that," I told him. "If you would read page thirty-seven of *Robert's Rules of Order*, you would find halfway down the page that you need a two-thirds majority."

He got up twice more suggesting procedures that were out of order, and because I knew my *Robert's Rules*, he had to back down both times. The congregation did everything but stand up and yell their approval. I could feel the emotional release as this congregation was set free from a man who had bound the church for fifteen years. In my ten years at that church, he never again disrupted a congregational meeting.

"If you want to kill any idea in the world today," said well-known engineer and manufacturer C. F. Kettering, "get a committee working on it." More than likely, Kettering had been on a few too many church committees.

But meetings don't have to be counterproductive. Church meetings graced by the presence of the Holy Spirit and led by influential leaders with people skills can be some of the most meaningful, rewarding times in church life.

*PART FOUR*
# Time to Rest

*Long before God called me to be a pastor, God has called me to be a responsible and loving human being.*
— *Steven McKinley*

CHAPTER TEN
# Fitting Ministry into the Family

I was a young pastor, recently called to serve as solo pastor of a medium-sized congregation that had grown "stale." I threw myself wholeheartedly into the challenge, using all my skills and energy to lead the congregation into a lively commitment.

I was also a young father. Our first-born daughter was about 2 years old at the time. I do not remember the exact circumstances. I only remember that it was a typically busy time in the life of the congregation. I attended meetings late into the night and returned to the office early in the morning.

The parsonage was only a sidewalk's width away from the church, so most days I came home for lunch. One day at lunch, my wife reported to me a question our daughter had asked that morning.

"Does Daddy ever come home and sleep with you any more?"

By the time I would get home evenings, our 2 year old was asleep. When she awoke the next morning, I was already back to the office. In her beautiful innocence, she wondered if I *ever* came home for the night.

In recent years, "family values" have become a major political topic. Though we might not agree on the definition of family values or on which political program bests supports them, we pastors tend to agree that the American family today is in crisis. We see it in the people we serve: in marriages breaking up, in children rebelling, in teenage suicide, in families torn apart by busyness.

I have decided that if I'm going to decry the sorry state of the modern family, I had better first start with myself. Though I've been tempted to think otherwise, workaholism is no more commendable in the parish pastor than it is in a rising junior executive. This is one thing my daughter's innocent question helped me realize.

Long before God called me to be a pastor, God called me to be a responsible and loving human being. And he graced me by giving me a wonderful family with which to live out that calling. While God's grace can certainly cover the sin of neglecting that call, I still long to live up to it and to my call to minister to a congregation.

### How Do We Do It?

Over the years, I've found several patterns that work for me, assuring I carry out my family and church responsibilities.

1. *Creative family time.* Responsible pastors work long and hard hours. But our schedules still offer us the great advantage of *flexibility*. Pastors do not punch time clocks. We do not report to supervisors who want to make sure we are on duty from 8:00 A.M to 5:00 P.M. every day. We can take advantage of that flexibility to do things with our families that other people are not able to do.

Early in my ministry I came to terms with the fact that I would be attending meetings or making calls three or four nights every week — and sometimes five or six. Usually I am out the door soon after supper. And it is not unusual for me to leave the rest of the family still at the table.

So I decided to begin coming home around 4:00 each afternoon. When our children were young and in school, that meant I arrived home about the same time they did. That's when we had our family time — before supper, not after. I routinely head to the office by 8:00 A.M. at the latest. If my work load is particularly heavy, I will get there by 7:00 A.M. This does not disrupt our family life. Everyone is getting up and going. Our youngest daughter catches her school bus at 6:45 every morning, so there is no reason for me not to be ready to go when she is.

With my wife back in the work force and two of our children grown, I use this late afternoon block of time to visit with our youngest and to prepare dinner for the family. When my wife gets home, we eat together, and I can dash out the door in time for my evening commitments.

I've come to look forward to this late afternoon routine, especially to making dinner. Everybody has bad days, and sometimes making dinner is my most concrete accomplishment.

When our children were still in school, I always made a point to schedule in parent conferences and special school events. If they were in a program at 2:00 P.M., they could count on my being there. Our children appreciated that. Many other parents could not be there. I can honestly say I never missed a school program or a parent conference.

At the beginning of every school year, I got into the habit of going through the school calendar and putting the one- or two-day school breaks into my calendar. I then kept those days as free as possible.

And before my wife returned to the work force, we used my flexibility to make time to be together. Many times we played a round of afternoon golf or ate lunch at our favorite restaurant or went shopping. Particularly in the summer, we made use of my flexibility, when the church calendar was less crammed.

2. *The board is not an ogre.* Invariably the church's schedule runs head-on into the family's schedule. I have found assertiveness — letting people know my family comes first — is sometimes worth the trouble.

When our oldest daughter was a junior in high school, she was elected to the National Honor Society. What a thrill for her and us! But the induction of new honor society members was scheduled for the same night as the monthly meeting of our governing board.

I stewed over that one for some time. Finally I went to our board president, explained to her our circumstances, and informed her I would miss that month's meeting. The resistance I had expected did not materialize. She sent me off with her best wishes and congratulations. The board met. Productive business was transacted. But I, the pastor, was not there. I was sitting in a high school auditorium, rejoicing with our daughter.

My own willingness to be assertive about my family responsibilities gives everyone else in the church the same freedom. As a matter of fact, we encourage our people to be protective about their family time. I accept the fact that I as pastor will be involved in church work three or four nights each week. That comes with the territory. But when I see the same people showing up for choir, adult classes, and committees, until they are spending three or four nights a week at church, I begin to worry. The church may be doing more to tear families apart than enabling them to be together. So we let our people know up front that missing meetings, when it allows them to be with their families, is perfectly acceptable to us.

3. *The accessible pastor.* Fred is an engineer, designing complex machinery to manufacture the products his company specializes in. Norma develops computer software. Todd is comptroller of his company. Jean assembles medical devices. They all do difficult and specialized work. Their spouses and children have only the vaguest understanding of what it is they do during their work days. Their families seldom see their workplaces. The people they work with are known to family members only by names. Their work worlds are totally separate from their home worlds.

My family belongs to the church I serve. They sometimes see

me doing my work. The church building is familiar to them. They know the people with whom I work. They have a basic understanding of what Dad does. They've heard my sermons, attended weddings and funerals, sat in classes I've taught.

They understand that sometimes Dad will get an emergency call to help someone in the congregation. They know that Dad talks with people to help them find solutions for their most pressing problems. While I respect confidentiality and do not reveal details of my counseling, they do know what counseling is, and that their Dad does it.

My work is accessible to my family. They share in it with me. They understand why I am sometimes sad, sometimes frustrated, sometimes elated. That they do brings us all closer together.

4. *Enough is enough even when it's not enough.* I drove into the familiar driveway of the congregational president. I walked up to the door, rang the bell, talked for a few minutes, handed him the keys to the church and the parsonage, exchanged hugs and handshakes, got back into the car, and drove away. Some weeks earlier I had announced my resignation, having accepted a call to another church. By the time I presented my church keys to the church president, the moving van was already bound for our new home.

That was ten years ago. I still remember the unique feeling that *everything* was done. The baton was passed to a new pastor. I had completed everything I was going to do as pastor of that church. My work in that place was finished.

That was the last time I had that feeling. A few days later, I started work in a new congregation, picked up a new baton, and since then have never ended the day with everything done. There is always another visit, another telephone call, another sermon or class to work up. I do have days when everything on my to-do list is checked off. But even then, I'm still aware of the things I should have put on my list, but did not.

That can drive me crazy — and make me compulsive. Through the years I've had to discipline myself to quit before I'm finished, to recognize there will always be more to do than I can get done in a day. For my own health and the health of my family, I've forced myself to walk away from the church at an appropriate time.

Of course, in the event of a scheduled appointment or emergency, I stay longer. But at the beginning of most days, I know when I will leave at day's end. When that time comes, I leave, whether I have done everything I wanted to that day or not. And besides, there is a good chance I'll be back in the evening.

5. *We don't have to do much.* It is easy for me to be less than honest with myself and with other people. I am dishonest when I excuse my lateness or my neglect of the family by saying, "I *had to* call on Mrs. Miller," "I *had to* finish the chapter I was reading," or "I *had to* finish the newsletter."

Did I really *have to?* Probably not. As a human being, I have to eat, sleep, and take care of bodily functions. As a pastor, I have to preach and lead worship at a specified time, attend the meetings of the governing board, and do a few other essentials. Beyond that, I do the things I do because I have *decided* to do them.

If I call on Mrs. Miller, it is because I have decided to call on Mrs. Miller. My decision may have been right; Mrs. Miller may have needed a call. But I decide when I am going to do it. The world would not have ended if I had skipped the call to Mrs. Miller. The cause of Christ would have endured, even if I had stopped in the middle of the chapter. There really aren't many things I have to do at any specified moment.

The schedule of my day is not something forced upon me. It is something I decide for myself. Therefore, my position as a pastor does not force me to neglect my family. I have the freedom to decide what portion of my time will go to my family and what portion of my time will go to my work.

I once visited a widow of a pastor soon after her husband's death. She expressed great sympathy for me as a father:

"You have to work such long hours that you never have time for your family. When our grown children came to their father's funeral, it was the first time in years they were inside a church. They always thought of the church as the enemy, something that took their father away from them. Now they'll have nothing to do with the church."

I felt sorry for her, for her children, for her late husband. But the hard truth was and is that the fault was not the church's. It was the fault of her husband, who would never be honest with himself.

6. *To each her own.* When I arrived to be pastor of one congregation, I was pursued by a ghost. My predecessor's wife had been the "perfect pastor's wife." When my predecessor made pastoral calls, she tagged along. She attended most church meetings, just to play hostess. She sang in the choir, attended all circle meetings, and filled in at the church office.

Her ghost chased me around for months. When I would show up to make a pastoral call or attend a meeting, a few questions on my wife's whereabouts arose. Every circle expected her to participate. When my wife did not show up at their meetings with me, the church's organizations were surprised. There were thinly veiled hints that these were the things a pastor's wife was supposed to do.

These are not the things my wife does — never has, never will. She is a dedicated Christian, committed to the local church, but she prefers to minister in her own ways, believing her best contribution to the church is to be a good partner in life with me. And that's all right with me.

As I manage my own time, I also try to manage the pressures put on my family to live up to someone's stereotype of a pastor's family. If I don't buy into that stereotype, my family doesn't have to shoulder that heavy burden.

In this case, I dealt with this ghost, first, by ignoring it. I brushed aside the pointed questions and overlooked the thinly veiled hints. I took every opportunity to praise my wife, to build her up in public, to let everyone know that I was absolutely delighted with the way she supported me and the ministry of the congregation.

Second, I trusted that people would eventually appreciate the ways my wife would contribute. For instance, she did a marvelous job of helping our altar guild get better organized and worked with a number of creative people in creating a beautiful set of banners for the congregation.

I knew the ghost was finally gone one afternoon when I stopped by a women's circle meeting. When I stepped into the kitchen to get a cup of coffee, *the* bearer of power of the group followed me. In our brief conversation, she made it a point to say, "I always resented the way our former pastor's wife followed him around, as though he couldn't be trusted to do things on his own."

## The Best Reason Why

I've set down some actions I have taken to fit ministry into my family and my family into the ministry. But as I reread what I have written, something is missing.

Call it joy.

Balancing ministry with family life is not a burden to me. I don't do it because it is the right thing to do. I do it because nothing in life gives me more joy, more sense of fulfillment, than the time I spend with my family. After twenty-five years of marriage, my wife still quickens my pulse with a smile or the touch of her hand — as much as she did when she was a blushing bride.

These thoughtful, sensitive, intelligent young adults our children have grown into are among my favorite people. Whether hashing over our work days with the older daughter, talking baseball with the middle son, or bowling with the younger daughter, I thoroughly enjoy spending time with them. Nothing is more fun than those times, which are now all too rare, when the entire family is home, sitting around the dinner table, playing a board game, watching a TV movie, piling into the car to go somewhere, or simply enjoying being together.

We do not live in Disneyland. We have our squabbles now and then, just like anyone else. But the good times are much more common.

I do not wedge my family into my schedule because it is my duty, my responsibility — even though it is. I do it because nothing in life makes me happier than the hours I spend with them.

## "I Was a Fool"

Several years ago I wrote an article on pastors and their families for a denominational clergy journal. Soon after that article appeared, I received a letter from a respected pastor who had retired not long before.

He was widely known and admired for being the powerful pastor of a large church. He had led his congregation through a period of incredible growth. Loved by his people, he was a recognized leader in denominational circles. He retired in a blaze of glory.

But his letter shocked me: "I was the model pastor. I was a slave to the church. I served the people. I neglected my family. I was a fool."

I think of his words now and then. I remember my young daughter's question: "Did Daddy come home and sleep with you last night?" I think of the alienated, embittered spouses and children of pastors I have known over the years, those who knew the church only as a rival, an enemy.

Such incidents speak to me the way Scrooge's ghosts spoke to him in Dickens's *A Christmas Carol*. They remind me that time is fleeting, that I still have a chance, but that chance will not be forever. They remind me of how precious my family is, of the responsibility I have to my family, of the delight I have enjoyed and have yet to enjoy.

*Instead of taxiing down the runway towards a three-month getaway, I embarked on a day-to-day hike through the wilderness of weariness — a sabbatical in the midst of work.*

— *Greg Asimakoupoulos*

CHAPTER ELEVEN

# Sabbatical in the Office

Emotional exhaustion, physical weariness, spiritual anorexia. Twelve years of task-oriented ministry had taken its toll. I was battling pastoral burnout, and I was losing. Ironically, the very week the Allied Forces were claiming victory in the Persian Gulf War, my own spirit was surrendering to battle fatigue.

As I prepared my messages for Holy Week, the cross of Good Friday became a symbol of my mental anguish. I was hanging lifelessly on the cross of depression, laboring to breathe under the suffocating weight of routine pastoral demands.

In a conversation with my superintendent, I confessed despair. He suggested a four-syllable remedy: sabbatical.

An extended time away from the never-ending responsibilities of the church (with full pay) was not a foreign concept to me. Two of my closest colleagues had been granted twelve-week sabbaticals the previous summer. For both, the experience involved travel, rest, family reunions, and solitude. No degree was pursued. No article published. No manuscript written. Yet each returned home focused, fresh, and infused with a renewed desire to preach.

In the midst of my melancholy, the thought of "getting away from it all" had presented itself as a welcome hope even before the superintendent's call. His endorsement fanned my flickering fantasy into a burning desire.

I approached members of the congregation whose support was unquestioned. I confessed my frayed state. I expressed my hopes that the church leadership might endorse a sabbatical leave.

Their responses were less than encouraging: "A sabbati —what?" "For how long?" "You'd still collect a check?" "You're kidding, right?"

Although mentally I had begun packing my bags, their negative reactions stalled my sabbatical flight on the runway. The word *sabbatical* did not translate into the vocabulary of my congregation, who are largely blue-collar workers and middle-management lifers. Even the one person with whom I had attended college (whose father was a university professor) protested.

"I know all about sabbaticals for educators," Jeff boasted. "But I've never heard of it in the ministry. Besides, if you take off for three months, the church's finances will plummet."

Jeff's words characterized the feelings of those I approached. My superintendent's prescription for emotional survival was viewed as an unjustified vacation. I felt betrayed. I thought my church cared for me. Resentment stirred my already troubled spirit.

The pressures of pastoral time demands include the need to find time away from things pastoral. Just as we need a day off weekly, I believe we need extended periods off, at least two to three

months every few years. But as I discovered, that isn't always possible. What then do we do?

Once my anger dissipated, I devised an itinerary for survival.
Instead of taxiing down the runway towards a three-month
getaway, I embarked on a day-to-day hike through the wilderness
of weariness. I developed what turned out to be twelve keys to
taking a sabbatical in the midst of work.

### Pack Only the Essentials

For as long as necessary, I learned to say no more than I said
yes. A wilderness hike is a survival course. It demands living lean.

Christian management consultant Fred Smith learned first hand
what it takes to survive: "I ought to be able to write down the two,
three, or four major things I simply cannot slight, and I must be sure to
work only on them. Everything else has to be pushed aside."

Realizing a sabbatical would not be forthcoming, I took the
initiative and informed the pastoral relations committee what areas
I would attend to for three months (and what areas I planned to
neglect). They agreed. The essentials in my backpack included worship planning, preaching, writing, and emergency pastoral care.

Office mail I normally would have opened and dealt with, I
stuck, unopened, in the boxes of board members. When a couple
phoned late one day and asked if they could meet me that night to
discuss their marriage problems, I made a judgment call: I decided
their problem was not an emergency and said we could schedule an
appointment (normally I would have forgone my planned family time
and counseled them that night). It turned out that the problem was a
temporary flare-up that passed, and we never needed to meet.

The weight of my pack proved just right.

### Secure a Reliable Guide

I sensed I should avoid at all costs solitary climbing along the
edges of burnout. Emotional exhaustion often disorients us. We
need others to point us in the right direction. I took the advice I had
given to scores of hurting people in my parish and sought out a
reputable Christian therapist. His penetrating questions and tested

observations provided weekly guidance as I trudged up the seem-ingly insurmountable mountains of ministry. I had the security that, no matter how lost I felt, he would help me stay on the trail.

I had to struggle against false guilt during this time of healing. For instance, though I feel called to write and find it fulfilling and therapeutic, I felt guilty about taking time away from church-related ministry. My "guide" assured me that writing was part of my call-ing, part of what my church supported me to do in its outreach to the larger world. Talking this through gave me a new sense of assurance and peace.

Guides come in all shapes and sizes. Not only did a therapist help me, so did my wife, a colleague across town, and even my church chairman. The only prerequisite for trustworthy guides: they need to provide unconditional acceptance that allows you to climb out of your pit at your own pace.

## Take Binoculars

I found it essential to take my eyes off my desk to daydream or drink in the beauty of God's creation at least once a day. It's so easy to fix my focus on the trail and forget the songbirds overhead that originally called me to ministry.

For six weeks I limited the length of my daily to-do list. Not everyone in the hospital got visited. Letters remained unwritten. Some phone calls weren't returned. And I recycled a newsletter devotional from two years previous instead of writing a new one. As a result I recaptured enough time to reflect on and rejoice in what I had accomplished. The field glasses of discretionary time allowed me to see the world that existed apart from next week's sermon.

## Pitch Your Tent Nightly

I gave myself permission to sleep in each morning for a week or two. Adrenaline can camouflage how tired we really are. I fig-ured that if I felt the need for a sabbatical, I most likely needed to catch up on my sleep.

Psychologist Archibald Hart of Fuller Seminary suggests a way to determine how much sleep your body demands: if you hide your alarm clock in your night stand for a week, your body will wake up on its own without artificial stimulation. When I followed his advice, I discovered how weary I was. Much of my depression was actually my body's muffled cry for rest. At first I felt guilty for sleeping in and watching the *Today Show* while sipping coffee (or catching a few warm rays of sunshine as I read the paper on the deck). But after two weeks of not meeting anybody for early morning meetings or worrying about what time I clocked in at the office, I got rid of both my guilt and the accumulating luggage under my eyelids.

### Grab Your Walking Stick

That's another way of saying, establish a realistic exercise routine.

My therapist suggested that my life was in need of balance. For me that meant incorporating an aerobic workout into my daily regimen. I'm not an athlete by lifestyle, and my body gave ready witness to the flabby truth. I began to walk briskly for an hour a day. (I could afford an hour because of my scaled-down demands.)

Ironically, that hour away from my desk was most productive. It gave me time to pray, which I hadn't been doing much of in my depressed state. Walking also gave me time to reacquaint myself with the satisfaction of muscle fatigue, to be alone with my thoughts, and to catch up on the news — I'd often wear my Walkman. After two months of power walking, I began jogging (I'm up to four miles a day and actually enjoy it).

I've discovered there is something refreshing about achieving personal goals, like exercise, that don't have to pass by the board first. Of all the steps I've taken to survive without a sabbatical, regular exercise was the most immediate salvation. At the end of the first week, I was sleeping better and awaking rested. After the second month, my head cleared considerably, and I felt more optimistic.

### Remember Your Whittling Knife

Making it through ministry requires making time for me, and that includes digging out my "whittling knife."

Some of my friends have dusted off their golf clubs or softball mitts. Others have dug out that old fishing pole or invested in a new tennis racquet. I chose to pursue a latent interest in photography, which soon became a meaningful way to express my often captive emotions.

With the pressures of people's problems, pessimistic pew sitters, and sermon preparation, factoring joy into my routine has worked well.

Call it a hobby. Call it a divine diversion. Call it whatever. I just call it fun and call it often. And I don't give up because of a busy signal. There will always be a legitimate excuse for not relaxing and having fun. But such excuses are no excuse. Recreation is a means of being re-created from within. Besides, who ever heard of a hiker who didn't pack a knife, harmonica, or camera?

### Carry Along a Hiker's Log

I journaled my journey. When emotions and thoughts held me hostage, I learned anew that a pen and notebook offered a way of escape. Getting my feelings onto paper relaxed their strangulating grip and let me look at the invisible. I've heard it said, "Thoughts untangle and make more sense when they pass through articulating finger tips."

In addition, as I looked back on previous documented difficulties, I better discerned my tendencies and God's faithfulness. My journal from seminary days reminded me that discouragement and drivenness have shared my berth before. As I reread my restless seminary journal, I found reason to believe God would rescue me once again.

I didn't follow a schedule or place demands on myself to journal. When needed, I used it as an emotional catharsis, not a diary, and usually for only about fifteen minutes at a time.

### Look Out for the Lookouts

Howard Thurman from Harvard Divinity School first introduced me to the concept of "minute vacations" in his book *The Inward Journey*. There's something to be said for a wee pause for our network of nerves to identify themselves and relax — reclining in a chair, feet on the desk, eyes closed, meditation. Three or four times a day, such an inner panorama helps recalibrate my perspective.

But minute vacations can be enlarged to include an afternoon of antiquing with your wife, a day at an art museum with your son, going away on a solitary retreat for a night or two to read and pray, or religiously taking a minivacation from work once a week —some call it a day off.

### Listen to the Waterfalls

Emotional exhaustion is often accompanied by apathy and dulled feelings; life loses its song. If music could make a difference for someone as tormented as King Saul, how much more for a pastor.

I incorporated my car stereo and boom box into my daily grind, turning on the music that fueled my feelings. I discovered my Walkman to be more than a source of news. It was my emotional jumper cable. Praise music and classical masterpieces, even the big-band sounds of the 1940s lifted my spirits. I cranked up the volume and luxuriated in melodies that ministered to my shriveled heart. The sounds of these alpine waterfalls helped keep this hiker on the hoof.

### Pull the Snapshots Out of Your Pack

I regularly update the photos on my desk. Those framed faces remind me whom I'm providing for, and that my provision is more than just bringing home the bacon; my wife and kids want the whole hog to hug and spend time with.

An occasional glimpse at those we love helps us focus on what ultimately matters (and it's not Mrs. Jones's hernia). Remembering my identity as a husband and father keeps me from being too compulsive about my role as pastor.

One night, when we were sitting around the dining room table, out of nowhere my seven-year-old daughter said, "I'm so happy when we're together as a family." That's positive reinforcement!

## Collect Firewood

In other words, I build altars of praise. I practiced the discipline of personal worship even when the desire to do so was absent. If ever an awareness of God is needed, it is in the blindness of burnout. On the mountain trail in the withering midday heat, the need for firewood is not as obvious as it will be come nightfall. It means doing what we don't feel like doing at the time.

When I annually explain the process of confirmation to our sixth-grade parents, I suggest that in confirmation we are laying the logs of truth in the fireplace of Christian community, so that when the Holy Spirit ignites a flame of faith, there is something to sustain a fire. That is similar to what I experienced in my private times before the Lord. Upon the cold hearth of my cold heart, I placed the logs found in poetry, music, silence, Scripture.

At first I was tempted to go through the motions of a routine quiet time. But my ability to fake it soon faded. I resisted benign devotions in favor of honest communication with God. No regimented Bible study, no protracted periods of prayer — at times just thoughtful sighs and audible groans in an empty sanctuary were the only twigs I could find. But God was there. He also found me in King David's diary of depression, the Psalms. He even spoke to me through a couple of those radio Bible teachers our congregations compare us to. Through simple and sincere expressions of friendship with the Father, I collected a pile of logs for when the flame of passion would return.

As of now, those spiritual flames are still in the process of returning. It's been a slow recovery, with emotional restoration coming far more easily than spiritual. Still, I feel more loved and accepted by God than at any time in my ministry.

## Keep in Contact with the Lodge

When paraplegic Mark Wellman climbed Half Dome in Yosemite National Park last fall, he maintained regular contact with the park lodge. His supporters waited at the valley floor with baited interest because of the precarious challenge facing their friend. Mark complied with their need to know how he was doing and used his walkie-talkie often.

I chose to share with my board my ups and downs. I disclosed my own need for pastoral care from a therapist. I distributed articles on the phenomena of pastoral burnout and ministerial stress. I also shared some of my struggles with the church, though not enough to undermine my credibility.

A few critics have pointed to my nonsabbatical sabbatical as evidence of my shortcomings. Our church had been going through a conflict of sorts before and after this period. My candid approach of dealing with my needs lost me a few more credibility points with them.

But for the vast majority in our church, I gained credibility. Many people have repeatedly thanked me for handling the situation as I did, and they have been more open about their own struggles as a result. If I were to do it all over again, I wouldn't change a thing.

*Doing important-but-not-urgent things can make us better pastors and better persons.*
                                        — *Steven McKinley*

# Feeling Good about the Non-Urgent

---

It was a Friday night, 6:15 P.M. I sat in my car waiting for the green arrow so I could turn left into the church parking lot.

A stream of cars heading north paraded past me, away from the city. Many were pulling boats, a clear sign they were headed for a weekend at "the lake." The golf clubs in the back seats of others suggested they were heading for the Friday night league at a nearby golf course. Still other cars were driven by commuters whose faces showed relief. The busy workweek was over. The weekend was here.

Or so I fantasized.

I was heading for a wedding rehearsal, then a rehearsal dinner. I knew I wouldn't see home before 10:00 P.M. Most of my Saturday would be tied up with the wedding and reception. Sunday morning there would be the usual three worship services, then worship at two local nursing homes in the afternoon, and an orientation session for new church members that evening.

As I waited for the light to turn, watching the cars passing me, I felt envious, depressed, maybe even bitter. Everyone else had the weekend free (at least, that's how I imagined it); I had a full weekend of work ahead.

I do not hate my work — far from it. The folks getting married were perfectly pleasant; the reception would be at one of our favorite places; Sunday morning worship is a joy, there is satisfaction in worship at the nursing homes, it is always exciting to welcome new members. But it was still work, and I was more in the mood for kicking back. I had already put in a solid week of work, without a day off. And when the next Monday morning rolled around, I would be at my desk.

### Why the Urgent Tyrannizes

What is it that keeps us pastors so earnestly plugging along? Why do we live urgently, ignoring our own bodies, spirits, families, and relationships — all for the sake of our work (or so we say)? After I reflected on my own drivenness, I came up with several reasons.

1. *What will "they" think?* I assume they would think less of me if they found out I wasn't at my desk. Avoiding that feeling is difficult. I feel uncomfortable when I bump into a member of my congregation at the golf course at two o'clock on a weekday afternoon — even if I had worked twelve hours the day before, spent 8:00 A.M. to 1:00 P.M. earlier that day on church business, and planned to be back at church for an evening meeting.

But would they really think less of me? Some might. Some might not. After all, "they" are something I sometimes create in my own mind. When I ask myself, *What would they think?* what I am often asking is *What would I think?* I take my expectations of myself and project them onto the people I serve.

Over the years, when I've dared to raise this with members of my congregations, I've found invariably they're not nearly as demanding of me as I am of myself. They really don't care if I take time off. In fact, they expect it. They might not stand over me weekly, insisting I take one day of rest each week, but they do expect me to be responsible enough to do that on my own.

And if they *did* get irritated with me for taking an afternoon on the golf course, so what? Every congregation has a few people who will never be satisfied with the pastor. Saint Paul has a few not-so-nice words for those trying to be "people pleasers," rather than "God pleasers."

*2. The work ethic.* Our teenage daughter, Meg, is mentally handicapped. One afternoon I wanted her to help me prepare a congregational mailing, the kind of work she can do well. When I raised the topic with her at lunch, however, Meg said she didn't want to work that afternoon.

Then I did a terrible thing about which I still feel guilty. I asked her to bring me her Bible. When she did, we looked up 2 Thessalonians 3:10: "While we were with you, we used to tell you 'Whoever refuses to work is not allowed to eat' "(TEV).

Meg takes her Bible seriously; she also takes eating seriously. No more argument. She worked that afternoon. And ever since, when she or some other family member tries to avoid work, she occasionally refers to that verse. This makes Meg a typical American Christian. We take that verse so seriously that it becomes in our minds an admonition to work *all the time.*

I subjected Meg to what is sometimes my underlying philosophy of work: I'd rather wear out than rust out. I've come to see this motto for what it is: self-righteous. Why? Either way, I'm out! It's like saying, "I'd rather drive my car 100 MPH than 10 MPH." Neither one is a particularly good choice — and they are not the only choices. It is possible to drive my car 50 MPH. A car at 50 MPH will both get further than the car at 10 MPH and outlast the 100-MPH car.

There is a balance, a happy medium between wearing out and

rusting out. Embracing the work ethic need not mean we never do anything but work.

3. *The myth of indispensability.* You've probably heard the story of the small-town pastor who regularly walked away from his work to watch the trains that passed through his town. When asked why the trains fascinated him so, he answered, "I love to see something that moves without my pushing it!"

Often it seems like things happen in the church only when we prod and provoke and push them along — and maybe wind up doing the work ourselves. Always there are church people who need us to help them make their way across life's battlefields. Convincing ourselves we are indispensable is not difficult.

We are not. The time will come when I'll no longer serve my current congregation. It will survive my departure. The life of the church is carried along by the power of the Holy Spirit, not the skills and personality of any one pastor.

### Sharpening the Saw

Once we have broken the shackles of "their" expectations, the relentless work ethic, and the myth of indispensability, we're ready not only to grant ourselves time off but to start feeling good about doing the non-urgent: prayer, reading, putting up our feet and dreaming, recreation, rest. Indeed, because doing important-but-not-urgent things can make us better pastors and better persons, we can feel good about indulging in the non-urgent.

For several years, I've given myself permission to spend time on the non-urgent. Recently I read a book that helped crystallize and clarify for me its importance: Stephen R. Covey's best-seller, *The Seven Habits of Highly Effective People.* Many of the ideas in the balance of this chapter are derived from Covey's book.

Covey tells this story: Suppose you were to come upon someone in the woods working feverishly to saw down a tree.

"What are you doing?" you ask.

"Can't you see?" comes the impatient reply. "I'm sawing down this tree."

"You look exhausted!" you exclaim. "How long have you been at it?"

"Over five hours," he returns, "and I'm beat! This is hard work."

"Well, why don't you take a break for a few minutes and sharpen that saw?" you inquire. "I'm sure it would go a lot faster."

"I don't have time to sharpen the saw," the man says emphatically. "I'm too busy sawing!"

This man's foolishness is apparent. But when the man with the saw is me, when I'm hip deep in work, claiming I'm too busy to sharpen the saw, it isn't so apparent to me. But by practicing some of the principles set down elsewhere in this book — delegating and prioritizing, for instance — we can make time to sharpen the saw.

Covey proposes that saw sharpening has four dimensions: mental, spiritual, physical, and social/emotional. Reading, prayer, exercise, being with friends, rest — these are ways of sharpening the saw. They are as essential as the work we do. They are, as a matter of fact, what makes it possible for us to do what we do. (I can't help remembering the famous quote of Martin Luther: "I'm so busy today that I don't have time *not* to pray.")

Taking time for saw sharpening is how we maintain what Covey refers to as the *P/PC* balance. *P* stands for *production*. As pastors, we are responsible for producing certain things: sermons, lessons, programs, the newsletter, spiritual direction, pastoral counseling, worship leadership.

*PC* on the other hand, stands for *production capability*, the ability to produce those things. In the story, the man in the woods is so geared to his production — cutting down the tree rather than taking the time to sharpen his saw — he is neglecting his production capability.

I can certainly identify with that. There have been times in my ministry (and probably will be again) when I have been so caught up in my production that I have ignored my production capability.

You know the scenario: one or two sermons a week, two or three adult classes, confirmation classes, four meetings; a funeral, a wedding, a cancer surgery, a fragile newborn; a weekend retreat, a newsletter to get out, a worship service to plan, that "must-go-to" denominational meeting, a few counseling appointments; start the day early, end it late, too busy for a day off — everybody has a week like that now and then.

But sometimes a week like that is followed by another like that, and another, and another. I find myself snapping at my family, flinching when the telephone rings, laboring to produce a sermon that does not have my heart in it, wondering if I really have anything to offer the people I meet. When that happens, I've ignored my production capability. As a result, I am working harder and harder, producing less and less.

### Structuring for a P/PC Balance

Covey proposes looking at the organization of our time via a "Time Management Matrix." This matrix is divided into four quadrants on the basis of *urgency* and *importance*.

Something that is urgent requires our immediate attention. If I'm in the office by myself, for example, and the telephone rings, it is urgent. Something that is important, on the other hand, might *not* require my immediate attention, but it does contribute substantially to my priorities.

In *quadrant I*, Covey places that which is both urgent and important. If the church custodian informs me that the sanctuary is on fire, that is both urgent and important! If the hospital calls to tell me that a child from the congregation was just struck by a car and is in critical condition — that is both urgent and important.

In *quadrant II*, Covey places that which is not urgent but is important. The care of my own spiritual life, for example, may not be urgent, but it is important. Sitting down with the rest of the church staff to plan a special series of Lenten services may not be urgent (as long as I do it, say, before February 1), but it is important. Much of the professional reading we do is not urgent, but it is important.

In *quadrant III*, Covey places that which is urgent but not important. If I'm alone in the office and the telephone rings, it is urgent. But if the call is from a firm trying to interest me in doing a new church pictorial directory and my church just finished doing a church directory, it is not important. Often telephone calls, visitors, mail, and other requests make themselves sound urgent without being important.

It was Good Friday at 11:00 A.M. We were winding down from the celebration of Holy Communion on Maundy Thursday, taking care of the last-minute details for the Good Friday service, and making certain everything was ready for Easter Sunday. I was polishing the Easter sermon and anticipating home services of Holy Communion with several of our shut-ins that day.

All of a sudden, my office doorway darkened, and Randy emerged.

"Pastor," he said, "I need to talk to you right now."

"Fine, Randy, come on in. What's up?"

"Well, I've been thinking about the congregational golf tournament we have every August. I think we should have trophies this year, and my wife and I would be willing to donate them. But I'd like to know what you think of the idea and what we should put on the trophies. I have the day off today, and I'd like to get everything taken care of."

Randy's appearance in my office was *urgent*. He wanted attention right away. But ordering trophies for an August golf tournament is definitely not an important part of my April priorities — definitely a quadrant III moment! But I must tell the truth. I did, in fact, plan the trophies that day. I'm not proud of it, but I did it.

Even when that urgency does not correspond to importance, it is hard for us *not* to respond to urgency. Since urgency has a way of getting our adrenaline pumping, many of us thrive on emergencies and feed on urgency. But feeding on urgency can make us neglect the more significant nutrition of importance.

In *quadrant IV*, Covey places that which is neither urgent nor important. We call it trivia. The trivial can become alluring, an escape from the day's pressures. Few of us avoid quadrant IV totally. I confess to having a quadrant-IV machine in the family room of our house. It is called a television set. Of course, there are times when the television set brings me something urgent (a tornado warning) and/or important (a debate between presidential candidates). But most television programming is neither urgent nor important. It might be entertaining, and there is nothing wrong with entertainment as such, but it is not important.

A few years ago, I had lunch with a pastor named Earl. Those of us who were his neighbors heard rumors that things were not going well for Earl in his congregation, that his church members were unhappy with him. During lunch, I began to sense the reason. Earl's conversation was packed with reports on the guests Phil Donahue had on his program last week and the incredible plots of some of the daytime soap operas. It became clear that Earl was spending an inordinate amount of time in front of his TV set!

We all visit quadrant IV from time to time. But when we start to live there, we've got problems.

## Living in Quadrant II

In keeping with Covey's advice, I've made it my goal to spend as much time in quadrant I — the urgent and important — as I have to, and as much time in quadrant II — the non-urgent but important — as I can.

I try to be discerning about quadrant III — the urgent but not important — mistaking urgency for importance can be tempting. I do visit quadrant IV — neither the urgent nor important (as when one of my favorite teams is playing a crucial game) — but I refuse to live there.

Spending time in quadrant II — the important but not necessarily urgent — can make me a better preacher. I've always admired those preachers who have a keen insight into a complex portion of Scripture, a good quote, an illumining story. But powerful sermons don't happen by accident.

I've been playing golf since I was a teenager. I love the game, but I've never gotten very good at it. I admire those golf professionals who play the game close to par. Each year the LPGA — Ladies Professional Golf Association — plays a tournament in our area. Last summer I went to one of their practice rounds.

When I arrived early in the morning, some of our nation's finest women golfers were on the practice tee. I watched a while then walked over to the practice green to watch others putt. Then I headed onto the course and followed a group around the first nine holes. When I returned to the clubhouse, I checked the practice tee again, and some of the same women were still there — three hours later.

Then I walked the second nine holes. After those nine holes, I found that many of the women who had been on the practice tee earlier in the day were now working on their putting, and vice versa. They weren't playing that day, but they were practicing — for hours!

Practicing was not an urgent task for them that day, but it was an important task. This experience made clear to me why they are great golfers and I am a duffer: practice. They work at it, constantly. I just step up to the first tee and assume that I should be able to play as well as they do.

Much of the difference between the great preachers and average preachers may be the time taken for study, reflection, prayer, and reading. This is not time spent grinding out the sermon for next Sunday, but rather it is time spent sharpening the saw, a quadrant II activity. When the time comes for actual sermon preparation, they are sharp.

Sharpening the saw — spending time in quadrant II — includes the kind of mental and spiritual sharpening described above. It also includes the social/emotional and the physical.

Recent ministry studies have highlighted the tendency of some pastors to be "Lone Ranger" types, seeking to carry out their work in isolation from partners and colleagues. That often leads the Lone Ranger to get saddle sore, to run down and burn out.

When I spend time with those whose professional adventures are similar to mine, we are each sharpened. Once a month I attend a lunch with pastors whose congregations are like my own. Many of them are facing the same issues I'm facing. Some months my urgent pressures make me wonder if I can afford taking the time to attend this meeting. But I do attend most months. I find that when I do, I am encouraged, even if it's only because I've shared my frustrations with others who understand them perfectly well.

Likewise, I am more effective when I care for myself physically. Some months ago, my energy on the wane, I could tell I was being less effective than I wanted. My wife suggested that perhaps arriving at the church office before seven every morning was not essential. I took her advice. I began sleeping one hour later each day and discovered I was getting more done than I had before.

When I shove a daily walk or ride on the exercise bicycle off the schedule, I lose my sharpness. When I never step away from work to play golf or go bowling or see a movie or go to a concert, I get "flat."

### The Telephone Call That Never Came

When a few years ago I decided to wean myself from the tyranny of the supposedly urgent to practice what I've just described, I braced myself for the fallout. I expected that at least some of my church members would be unhappy with me, that I'd hear complaints about what was *not* getting done. I wondered how long it would take to get the first phone call of complaint.

I'm still waiting. That phone call has never come. My most recent annual performance evaluation from the church council, in fact, was the best I've ever received. Apparently my people are affirming Covey's principle. Sharpening the saw and spending time in quadrant II can make you a more effective pastor.

*Time management is ultimately an exercise in humility not power.*

— Craig Brian Larson

# Epilogue

We hear it said that Jesus was never in a hurry. Of course, on occasion he did cat nap in the stern of the boat, presumably because ministry demands had cut into his sleep the night before. And he stayed up late, sometimes all night, to catch up on prayers after hectic days of helping others. Even for Jesus, then, the "church calendar" was rarely clean and precise.

Likewise, a pastor's world has a way of shredding time management laws. One author of this book arrived a half-hour late for our appointment. Another returned his manuscript a month after deadline. Another had to forfeit vacation days to finish his chapters.

Not that these authors don't practice what they preach. As wonderful as unhurried ministry sounds, they know that to be faithful and effective in serving Christ, a leader must do many things well. And, alas, for even the best of us, people and problems defy absolute control.

Yet our schedules don't always stay manageable for a larger and — let's be honest — equally frustrating reason: God. Secular time-management maxims can intoxicate us with a false sense of control, of illusory power, but we who serve Christ are reminded repeatedly that God interrupts our plans. Insurance contracts call natural disasters "acts of God;" many schedule disasters are nothing less.

For pastors, then, time management is ultimately an exercise in humility not power. As stewards we employ all the wisdom at our disposal to live orderly and productively, yet never forgetting, as David said in Psalm 31, "You are my God. My times are in your hands."